How to Pass SELECTION TESTS

SECOND EDITION

MIKE BRYON & SANJAY MODHA

KOGAN PAGE

First published in 1991
Revised edition 1992
Reprinted 1994. Title changed to *How to Pass Selection Tests*
Reprinted 1995, 1996, 1997
Second edition 1998
Reprinted 1999

Kogan Page Limited
120 Pentonville Road
London N1 9JN

British Library Cataloguing in Publication Data

A CIP record for this book is available from the British Library.

ISBN 0 7494 2697 7

Typeset by Saxon Graphics Ltd, Derby
Printed and bound in Great Britain by Clays Ltd, St Ives plc

Contents

We dedicate this book to
Nima Modha-Bhatti and Ella Schlesinger.

Foreword to the Second Edition

The idea for this book arose from our work in pre-employment training for some of the largest employers in the UK. Our work involved preparing people for the selection process of these organisations and the posts that they would go on to fill.

An essential part of the work involved preparing candidates for the selection tests used by these organisations. This experience led us to conclude that many people who fail the tests could in fact pass them. What is required is that they come to terms with their anxieties and prepare prior to the test.

The purpose of this book is to make available to a general readership the strategies developed while preparing candidates for the selection tests.

Since its publication in 1991, *How to Pass Selection Tests* has become a bestseller and proved of considerable help to thousands of people who face employers' tests. This second edition ensures that the exercises continue to help candidates prepare for the challenge of selection tests. It also indicates sources from which the reader may obtain further practice material.

1 Aims of the Book

Many companies and organisations use tests for selection purposes and for many people these tests represent a significant obstacle to obtaining the job or career of their choice.

The aim of this book is to inform readers about these tests and provide exercises so that they can practise before sitting a test. Over half the book comprises exercises that are relevant to some of the most common types of selection test currently in use.

Practice can result in significant improvements in performance in most sorts of test. It also boosts confidence and helps individuals to cope with nervousness. It makes individuals less prone to mistakes and ensures that the test is approached proficiently.

Information is provided about the history and nature of tests, and explanations are offered about why companies use tests and what they believe can be concluded from the results. Advice is also given about what to do if you fail.

2 General Information About Tests

History of Tests

The first standardised test of ability was produced in France at the beginning of the century by Binet. Initially, the tests were developed for use with children for diagnostic purposes.

It was not until the First World War that testing for adults really began. These tests proved to be valuable in selecting and allocating recruits for different types of work in the armed forces and also for identifying potential officers.

During the Second World War further advances in selection methods were made. Once again, the tests proved to be valuable in allocating different people to a variety of jobs or trades at different levels or grades.

There were certain advantages in using paper and pencil tests in groups (these are also applicable today in industry and commerce). First, it allowed a large number of people to be tested in one sitting. Second, it allowed people to be tested under the same type of conditions, ie the physical conditions and instructions could be standardised. Third, people could be allocated to jobs or trades for which they had the aptitude rather than simply being rejected or allocated to jobs on the basis of a simple interview – which can be very subjective.

The use of tests in the two wars played an important part in classifying large numbers of people. Since then tests have been developed and adapted for the needs of industry and commerce. Many organisations, particularly the larger ones, now regularly use selection tests because of the advantages referred to above and other advantages to which we shall refer in a later section (see page 19).

What are Selection Tests?

Selection tests, as the name suggests, are tests which are designed and used for the purpose of selecting and allocating people. The tests can be used in a number of situations; for example, in selecting people for jobs, in promoting or transferring people to other departments or jobs, and in certain types of course. They are also used in redundancy and career counselling and are known as psychometric or psychological tests.

Psychometric tests are one way of establishing or confirming an applicant's competence for the job. They can be useful provided they are reliable and valid for the job for which they are being used. Selection tests are standardised sets of questions or problems which allow an applicant's performance to be compared with that of other people of a similar background. For example, if you happen to be a graduate your score would be compared to those of other graduates, or if you have few or no qualifications your score would be compared to people who are similar to you, and so on. What this means is that the tests are norm referenced (the section dealing with results explains what this means – see pages 10–11).

Reliability and Validity

We said that tests can be useful if they are reliable and valid. So what do these two words mean in this context?

It is said that a test is *reliable* when consistent results are obtainable. For example, tests which contain ambiguous questions are likely to be unreliable because different people will interpret the questions differently, or even the same person may interpret them differently on different occasions.

Tests are said to be *valid* when they measure what you want them to measure. In personnel selection terms it means that a test must be related in some way to the known demands of the job if it is to be of any use. For example, it needs to be shown that a test score predicts success or failure in a given job.

Figure 2.1 illustrates the kind of relationship that ought to exist between test scores and job performance in which the higher the

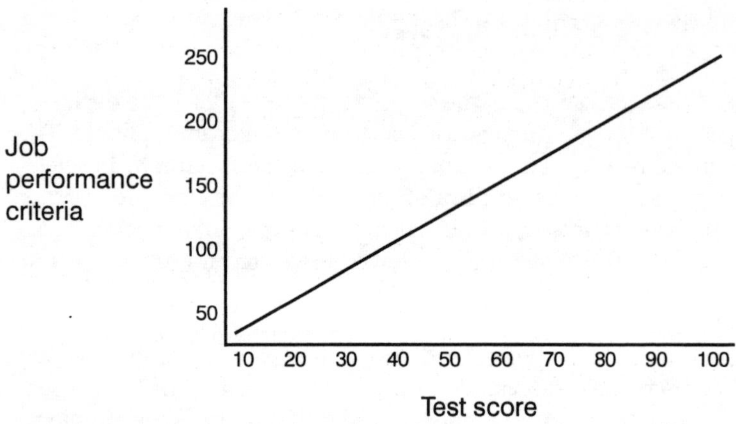

Figure 2.1 *A positive correlation between test scores and job performance*

test score the better the performance in the job. In reality, however, it would be almost impossible to find such a high positive correlation. This is because of the difficulties in measuring job performance in many, if not most, types of job.

Different Types of Test

In this section we shall look at the various types of psychometric tests and questionnaires that are used. These are attainment and aptitude tests (work sample and trainability tests are also aptitude tests) and personality and interest inventories.

Ability Tests

Ability is the most common aspect of a candidate which is subject to testing, either in the form of paper and pencil tests or some practical exercise. These practical tests are sometimes referred to as performance tests or work sample tests; another variation of these are the trainability tests. We shall deal with these later (see page 16).

Ability tests fall into two main categories: attainment tests and aptitude tests. Aptitude is having either a talent for a particular skill or the potential to acquire it. Attainment is the candidate's current skills and knowledge. It needs to be pointed out that the distinction between attainment tests and aptitude tests is not clear-cut. This is because a single test can be used to measure either attainment or aptitude.

Attainment tests

Attainment tests are those which seek to assess how much skill and knowledge an individual has. For example, an arithmetic test for supermarket cashiers measures attainment as long as it is used to measure arithmetic and not to measure performance as a cashier.

From an employer's point of view an attainment test may provide a better assessment than simply looking at a past record of achievements or non-achievements as the case may be. A standardised test of arithmetic or spelling may give a more reliable indication of relevant present ability than a comparison of school qualifications in maths or English.

From a candidate's point of view an attainment test score will say more to an employer than simply talking about his or her skills. This is particularly useful when the candidate does not possess many, or even any, qualifications.

Aptitude tests

Aptitude tests are used to predict the potential of an individual for a particular job or a course of study. However, as mentioned above, it is not easy to separate tests of potential from tests of attainment because all forms of test assess the person's current skills and knowledge. But the results of that assessment may then be used in a variety of ways. For example:

- to highlight the individual's strengths and weaknesses
- to provide career counselling
- to predict success in a job or course.

Work sample tests

Work sample tests are no different from the paper and pencil aptitude tests except that they are practical. They are a miniature version of the job in question. The tasks encompass the main or major elements of a job. They are called work sample tests because that is the main purpose, hence they are sometimes referred to as performance tests.

Trainability tests

Another variation of the work sample test is the trainability test. Trainability testing is a method of assessing applicants' potential for learning new skills in a particular area by carrying out a practical exercise.

Personality Questionnaires (Tests)

Many people refer to personality inventories or questionnaires as tests. This, however, is misleading because to talk about personality questionnaires as tests implies that there is a pass or fail score, which is not the case.

Personality is something that everyone talks about. You often hear people talking about someone having a 'great personality', but what exactly is it?

There is no one theory or definition of personality with which all psychologists agree, but most personality questionnaires aim to identify certain stable characteristics. They are based on the assumption that the responses to be given will be a representative sample of how an individual will respond in a given social situation, particularly the one in which the selector is interested, ie the organisation or department in which that individual may be working.

The main characteristics that personality questionnaires aim to identify in an individual are:

Extroversion	Introversion
Tough minded	Tender minded
Independent	Dependent
High self-confidence	Low self-confidence

Interest Inventories (Tests)

Strictly speaking, interest tests like personality tests are not tests at all, because they are not about obtaining a good or a bad score, or about passing or failing. It is for this reason that they are usually referred to as interest inventories or interest questionnaires. The aim of these interest inventories is to find out an individual's interest in particular occupations.

Interest inventories cover interests in activities such as:

Scientific/technical	–	how and why things work or happen
Social/welfare	–	helping or caring for people
Persuasion	–	influencing people and/or ideas or selling goods and services
Arts	–	designing or creating things or ideas
Clerical/computing	–	handling data, systems

The use of interest inventories is limited compared to, say, aptitude tests in the selection of applicants. This is because the inventories appear, at least on the face of it, easy to fake. For example, if a person is applying for a position as a clerk, he or she may deliberately indicate a stronger interest in tasks related to the office environment.

The interest inventories are probably most useful in vocational guidance where one assumes that people are less likely to fake them.

Fair and Unfair Discrimination

All good tests discriminate! That, after all, is the purpose of the test. However, this discrimination should be on the basis of ability, and so is fair and legal discrimination. If the tests, or the way in which they are used, discriminate on the basis of sex or race it would be unfair and possibly even illegal under the Sex Discrimination Act 1975 and the Race Relations Act 1976.

It does not matter whether the unfair discrimination is intentional or unintentional. However, the Acts do not explicitly refer to testing. The implication of the two Acts is that if the use of the tests (or other selection methods) results in proportionately more women or members of the ethnic minority communities 'failing' the test and as a result not being taken on and the use of the test cannot be justified, this may be unfair discrimination. The onus of proof is on the employer to justify the use of the test.

For example, if an employer sets a condition (let us say a test score of X or above) and a larger proportion of women or ethnic minority groups fail to meet this condition, compared to men or the ethnic majority group, the employer may be required to show that this condition is necessary. If the use of the test can be shown to be justified, the result would be fair discrimination.

When an employer uses tests to select employees, it is on the understanding that the test will differentiate between those candidates with and those without the appropriate skills, knowledge and potential. A test which does not differentiate between the level of abilities in candidates is of no real value to the employer. It is important to the employer that the right person is chosen for the right job. It is equally important to the candidate that it is the right job for him or her. Otherwise the candidate may not be happy in the job or, even worse, he or she may not be capable of doing the job, which can be very demoralising.

Fair discrimination is about distinguishing between people, based on their abilities and aptitudes. These must be shown to be related to the job for which the tests are being used. What this means in practice is that if an employer uses a particular test to identify a given set of abilities and aptitudes, these must be shown to be necessary to do the job. For example, it may need to be shown that high scorers do well in the job in question and that low scorers do not.

We mentioned the Sex Discrimination Act and the Race Relations Act. These two Acts, which have much in common, have identified two types of discrimination: direct and indirect.

Direct discrimination is where an employer treats someone favourably because of his or her sex, colour or ethnic background. Such discrimination is unlawful.

Indirect discrimination is where an employer sets a condition which a large proportion of a particular group fail to meet, eg women or people from ethnic minority groups. This type of discrimination could be held to be unlawful if the condition set by the employer is not necessary or justified.

Why Companies use Tests

There are a number of advantages to companies and other organisations in using psychometric tests. These include:

1. Where an organisation receives a large number of applications, and because most selection tests are paper and pencil type, applicants can be tested in large groups. This, of course, is much more cost-effective.
2. The recruitment and selection process can be a costly affair, particularly if there is a high turnover of staff because of bad selection decisions, not to mention any other disruptions that may be caused. Thus it is in the interests of the company to choose the right people for the job. The use of tests can help in this process, provided that the tests are both valid and reliable.
3. Tests can also lessen subjectiveness in assessing the applicant's potential to develop his or her aptitude for a particular job. The lessening of subjectiveness in the selection process is also an advantage for applicants.
4. The use of tests with other selection procedures can lead to better and fairer decisions on the part of the employer.

Test Conditions

Most tests are conducted under strict 'examination' type conditions. The main reason for this is to ensure that all candidates, at all times, are tested in the same manner. This is so that no group being tested is either advantaged or disadvantaged in terms of receiving the test instructions.

The process followed will be laid down by the test publishers. However, the majority of tests are likely to be conducted in the following way:

1. All candidates will be sitting facing the test administrator.
2. Candidates will be provided with all the materials necessary, such as pencils, eraser, answer sheets, rough paper (if allowed by test publisher).

3. The tester will explain the purpose of the test(s) and also inform candidates how the test will be conducted.
4. The tester will read the instructions to be followed for the test. These instructions may also be written on the test booklet, in which case they should be read at the same time. In some tests the candidates are left to read the instructions by themselves. The reading time may be included in the test time or extra time may be given.
5. For the majority of tests, if not all, there is a strict time limit which the tester will adhere to. The tester may use a stopwatch; don't be put off by this.

   Interest inventories and personality questionnaires do not usually have a strict time limit, though candidates are asked to complete them as quickly as possible.
6. Many tests have example questions. In some tests the candidates are asked to attempt these, while others have them already completed. In any case, their purpose is to ensure that the candidates understand what is required of them.
7. In most tests, candidates are given the opportunity to ask questions. If you do not understand what is required of you, you should seek clarification. You should not feel intimidated about asking questions, no matter how trivial the question may seem to you. The chances are that there are other people who have similar questions but who haven't plucked up enough courage to ask them. So the motto is – ask; you have nothing to lose!

How the Results are Interpreted

So far we have talked about different types of test. Now we need to address the issue of what happens once you have taken the test.

Naturally, they are scored; that is, they are marked. Once scored, the correct answers are added together. The result is called a raw score. If there is more than one test all the raw scores are noted. A set of tests is called a battery of tests.

The raw score does not really mean anything on its own. This is because it does not tell us whether it is a good or a bad score. Let us assume that candidate A gets 30 questions right out of a possible 50. So candidate A has a raw score of 30. If the test is easy and most people who are similar to him or her would have scored around 40, A's score is bad. On the other hand, if the test is a difficult one and most of the other people would only have scored around 20, candidate A's score is a good one.

Thus, in order for the scores to be meaningful, we have to compare the individual's score with that of a similar group of people. We would then be able to say that, compared to those people, this individual is either average, above average or below average. We make this comparison by using what are called norm tables. Norm tables tell us how other people have scored on a test. The group with whom we would compare an individual's score is called a norm group and test norms are the norm group's scores. In a norm referenced test the raw scores are compared with a norm group.

3 What to Do if Invited to Sit a Test

Why Practice Helps

If you and some friends were invited to enter a competition to change the wheel of a car in the shortest possible time and your team had practised, you would expect to be faster as a result. Your team would be less prone to mistakes and you would set about the task in a far more effective way.

Practice can lead to improvements in performance in most sorts of test, including those used by companies during selection. By how much your score might improve depends on a number of things. One is the amount of practice that you undertake; another is the quality of the material on which you practise (it must be similar to the real test). An important variable is whether you have had much previous experience of selection tests. The candidate who is new to tests stands to show the most improvement, while someone who has had lots of test experience may show little or no improvement.

The most important single factor that will decide by how much you improve your score through practice is you! To improve, you have to be motivated. From our experience, doing well in a selection test is not simply a matter of intelligence or aptitude: you also have to try hard and you must have a certain amount of self-confidence.

As we have said, not everyone will show an improvement; if you have taken lots of selection tests you may show little or none. Equally, anyone who is a poor reader or weak at maths may need to attend literacy or numeracy classes before any noticeable improvement. But for many, practice will make a significant contribution and in some cases will allow you to pass what you would otherwise have failed.

Whether practice will make the difference in a particular instance depends on where you are starting from. If you would have passed anyway, practice may only help you to obtain a slightly higher score. If you would have failed with a very low score, you may not be able to improve enough to pass, no matter how much you practise. However, you may be among the large number of candidates who fail a selection test by only a few marks and 12 to 16 hours' practice may mean that, instead of failing, you pass.

The way to look at it is this. What have you got to lose? Spending, say, two hours a night for six nights practising for a test can only help and it might make all the difference.

There is evidence to suggest that practice does help. For example, a woman who had twice failed the Civil Service test for Administrative Assistants, and had been trying to get an administrative job in the Civil Service for over a year, enrolled on a course that provided a total of five days' test practice. At the end of the course she sat the test and passed.

Make a Decision

You have to decide how much you want the job. If you decide that it is something you really want you should make up your mind to attend the test! It is not unusual for as many as 40 per cent of the candidates to fail to show up on the day. You are also going to have to set aside some time to prepare for the test.

If, in your search for work, you have experienced a lot of rejection it is going to take courage to make the level of commitment that we ask.

Establish a Clear Idea of the Test Demands

The company or organisation that invites you to take a test will most likely include with the invitation a test description. This is an important source of information. If you do not receive such a description, telephone the company and ask if you can be sent details.

It is essential that you establish from the test description a clear idea of what the test involves and select exercises with similar demands. To help ensure that you do indeed have a clear idea, try the following exercise.

Familiarise yourself with the test description to the point at which you are able to describe in your own words each section of the test. For example, you ought to be able to state how many sections the test consists of, how long you are allowed for each section and what you have to do in each. If you are unable to do this you are not sufficiently familiar with the test description, so continue to read it to yourself until you can describe each section in your own words.

Ask someone else to read the description sent by the organisation and explain to him or her your account of what you are going to have to do. If your friend accepts your account of the test, you've got it.

Seek Out Relevant Material

If the test involves maths and English exercises the majority of the material in this book will be of use. However, if the test is designed to measure, for example, co-ordination, dexterity, perceptual skills or abstract mental reasoning, you will need to obtain additional material. Likely sources are books with exercises purporting to measure IQ (intelligence quotient) or offering an assessment of aptitude. Libraries and career services may be able to lend you copies. If the test measures specialist knowledge seek out textbooks on the subject, especially those that end sections with questions and answers. Libraries of colleges of further education may be a good place to begin your search. If you are not a student you will probably not be allowed to borrow books, but no one should mind you using the library for reference purposes.

Prepare a Programme of Work

Once you have a clear idea of the test demands and sufficient practice material you need to plan when and where you are to practise.

You should practise for no more than two hours at a time and allow some time fairly close to the test. The benefits of practice are short-lived so practise right up to the day before the test. Although some is better than none, you should aim to undertake a minimum of 12 hours, and perhaps as much as 20 hours, of practice. The factor that will probably decide how much practice you do will be the amount of relevant material that you can obtain.

Always work somewhere quiet and don't listen to music or watch television at the same time. Your programme of work ought to look something like this:

You are notified that you are going to have to sit a test.

You undertake a study of the test description. (2 hours)

You search for relevant practice material.

You undertake a series of two-hour practice sessions. (10 to 18 hours)

You take the test.

Coach Yourself

Work through the material that you have obtained at your own pace without consulting the answers. Then go over it with the answers, trying to work out why the answer is the one given, rather than simply seeing how many you have got right; that way you are learning. Put the material aside and move on to other material; after a few days go through the original material again, this time against the clock (you might give yourself a minute an exercise). By following this method you will go over the material three times under a combination of conditions.

The Night Before the Test

Lack of sleep or illness will affect your score detrimentally. You need to get a good night's sleep before the test. If you are unwell telephone the organisation to see if you can sit the test at a later date. Do not drink alcohol before a test.

Test Anxiety

Do you get worried before taking a test?

Do you tend to think you are not doing well while taking a test?

Test anxiety is quite a common problem for most people. The only difference is the degree to which people worry. Generally, it has been found that a slight amount of anxiety is a good thing; however a large amount can be detrimental.

Too much worry and too many negative thoughts can draw attention away from the task in hand – that of taking the test – and thereby disrupt performance. On the other hand, a little anxiety is beneficial: it will help you to be more alert and help your performance.

If you are one of those people who worry too much and have negative thoughts about your performance during a test, you will need to learn how to relax. You will also need to be more positive. After all, failing a test is not the end of the world – though it may seem like it at the time!

Test Strategies

How you conduct yourself during the test is of utmost importance. There are a few golden rules.

Probably every test paper in the country advises the candidate against spending too long on a particular question. It is good advice. If you do not think you are going to be able to answer a question, move on to the next and if there is time come back to the questions that you have missed.

It is important that you place your answer in the correct place on the answer sheet or test booklet. If the test has an answer sheet separate from the questions, take particular care to check regularly that the question number corresponds to the number against your answer.

It is equally important that you indicate your chosen answer in the way requested. If the instructions ask you to, for example, tick the correct answer, make sure you do tick your choice rather than perhaps circle it or underline it.

Guessing sometimes pays. If the test is a multiple-choice paper and you do not know the answer, it may pay to guess. If, for example, you have to choose from four possible answers guessing would allow you to get, on average, one question in four right. Often you can improve on this average because you are sometimes able to recognise one or more of the suggested answers as incorrect.

Estimating sometimes helps in multiple-choice maths tests. Rather than working out inconvenient sums it is quicker if you round the amount up or down to a convenient number.

What To Do if You Fail

We have coached a lot of people through a range of selection tests and know for certain that failure does not necessarily mean that you are unable or do not have the ability to do the job. All it definitely means is that you failed the test! You may be perfectly able to do the job and pass the test if you took it a second or third time. The thing to do is not to give up.

Most companies will not tell you your score or allow you to retake the test straightaway. In some cases you are not allowed to retake the test for six months and you will have to re-apply which involves filling out the application form, and so on, all over again. This means that you have time to improve your English or maths so that you pass the test the next time.

It will help if, straight after the test, you sit down and try to remember as many of the questions as you can. Then go and find some exercises that remind you of the test. We suggested earlier the kinds of place you might find them.

Now test yourself on the examples that you managed to find; try to be honest and, if you do really badly, it may be that the only way you are going to improve is to attend classes at a college of further education. If you attended for a year you might obtain sufficient qualifications to exempt you from having to do the test again!

4 Some of the Most Common Types of Test

In this chapter, descriptions are given of some of the most common kinds of test and their demands are illustrated with examples. Further practice material is provided in Chapter 5.

You are most likely to encounter the following types of test:

Verbal reasoning. These are about how well you understand ideas expressed in words and how you think and reason with words.

Numerical reasoning. Like the verbal tests these aim to identify strengths in understanding, only in this case it is your strength in understanding and reasoning with numbers.

Diagrammatic reasoning. These deal with diagrams.

Mechanical reasoning. These deal with mechanical concepts.

Abstract reasoning. These seek to identify how good you are at thinking in abstract terms; ie dealing with problems that are not presented in a verbal or numerical format.

Clerical skills. These deal with checking and classifying data, speedily and accurately.

All the practice material provided in this book relates to the verbal, numerical and clerical types of test. If you are interested in diagrammatic tests of reasoning, you will find practice material in the following two books useful: *How to Pass Computer Selection Tests* and *How to Pass Technical Selection Tests* (both published by Kogan Page).

Nearly all these tests will have a time limit. But we have not imposed time constraints in this chapter because it is more important that you become familiar with the tests, and this is best done under relaxed conditions where you work at your own pace. Later you will find exercises that allow you to practise against time.

Verbal Tests

Tests That Measure Comprehension

These tests set out to establish if the candidate can demonstrate a level of understanding of written language. They can involve, for example, swapping or finding missing words, choosing between sentences, or identifying words that have the same or opposite meaning.

Tests That Assess Spelling

Most spelling tests require you to indicate which words in a list are incorrectly spelt. In some cases you are provided with a list of correctly spelt words from which you are able to check the spelling. You may have either to write or underline the correct spelling or look the word up on a correctly spelt list and write down the corresponding number.

Tests of Grammar and Punctuation

Grammar demonstrates the relations between words, while punctuation serves to divide and emphasise. It is quite common for tests of grammar and punctuation to examine also your command of spelling and comprehension.

Tests of Logical Thinking

These tests are intended to measure the candidate's ability to follow instructions or work out relationships between numbers, shapes, figures or statements and predict, for example, what comes next.

Numerical Tests

The purpose of these tests is to examine your grasp of the four fundamental operations of arithmetic: addition, subtraction, multiplication and division. We later refer to these as the four rules. Sometimes the test also investigates the candidate's handling of percentages and fractions. You are not usually allowed to use a calculator, slide rule or any other sort of aid. These tests may also require the candidates to apply their grasp of arithmetic to a series of practical situations or demonstrate their understanding by estimating the answers.

Tests of Clerical and Computing Skills

There are many tests that try to predict whether a candidate is suited to work with computers or as a clerk. For example, the tests investigate the candidate's ability to check information, follow coded instructions or rules, sequence events into a logical order and interpret flow diagrams.

Practice Examples

The following pages provide practice examples of some of the most common types of test. Do not worry if you cannot do some of the examples. If you get stuck ask someone to help. Answers are given on pages 130–133.

1. Verbal Tests That Measure Comprehension

A. Swapping words

Comprehension tests sometimes consist of single sentences or pairs of sentences that either do not read sensibly or have a word or words missing. You have to make the sentences sensible by swapping words or you have to complete a sentence by choosing words from a list.

Examples of swapping words:

Tick the two words that if swapped would make the following sensible.

you have to try test to do well in a hard.

Note that in this type of test you must only switch two words and from wherever you move the first word the other must go. Sometimes the question consists of two sentences one of which requires no revision.

Now try this example:

Tick the two words that if swapped would make the following sensible.

limit all tests impose a time virtually.

B. Finding missing words

If the sentence has a word or words missing you are expected to indicate which word or words are needed to complete the sentence, usually from a number of suggestions.

Examples of missing words:

The . . . sat on the . . .

A	B	C
mat cat	cat mat	mat mat

Answer

B

C. Locating words that mean the same or the opposite

Comprehension-type selection tests sometimes test a candidate's grasp of synonyms (words in the same language that mean the same) or antonyms (words that mean the opposite of each other or are contradictory). For example:

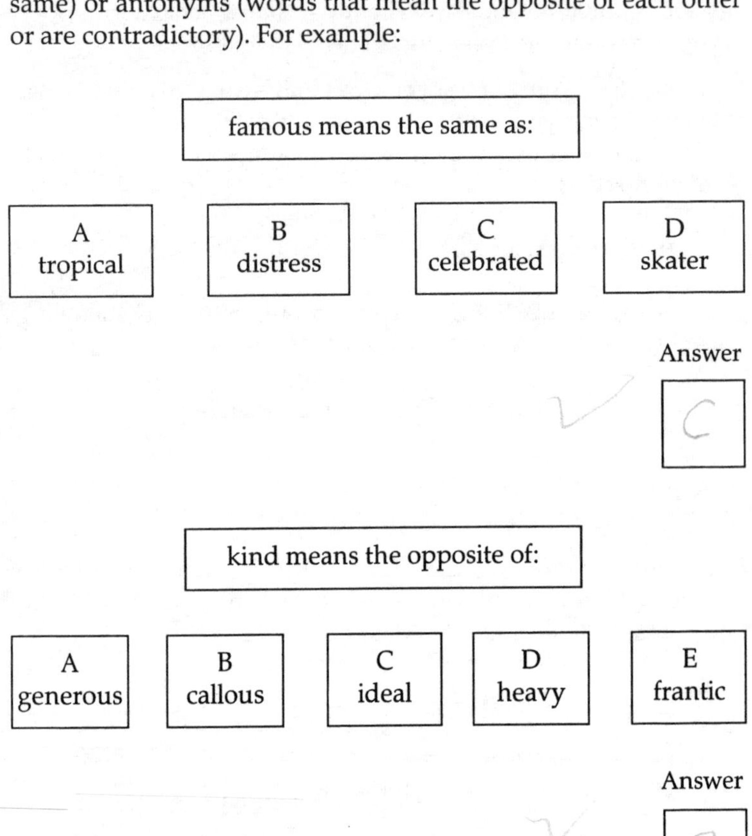

famous means the same as:
A
tropical
B
distress
C
celebrated
D
skater
Answer
C
kind means the opposite of:
A
generous
B
callous
C
ideal
D
heavy
E
frantic
Answer
B

2. Tests of Grammar and Punctuation

These tests often involve the candidate having to choose which of a number of sentences are correct or, alternatively, choose from a number of words, or pairs of words, which will correctly complete a sentence.

A. Choosing from a number of sentences

In each of the following two examples, choose which sentence is correct and place its letter label in the answer box:

(a) Where would you go to buy shoes.

(b) Where would you go to buy shoe?

(c) Where would you go to buy shoes?

(d) Where would you go to buy shoe's?

Answer

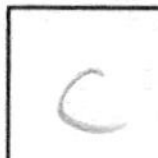

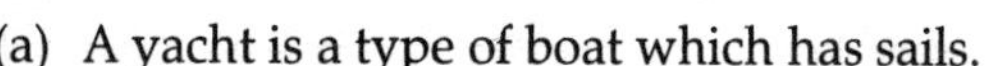

(a) A yacht is a type of boat which has sails.

(b) A yacht is a type of boat which that sails.

(c) A yacht is a type of boat who has sails.

(d) A yacht is a type of boat who that sails.

Answer

B. Choosing from pairs of words

Choose which pair of words correctly fits the spaces in the incomplete sentence.

Thomas and . . . . visit you yesterday.

A	B	C	D
me will	I will	me did	I did

Answer

Try this example:

. . . were . . . policemen to every protester.

A	B	C	D
Their too	There to	Their two	There two

Answer

3. Spelling Tests

These tests require you to identify which words are either correctly or incorrectly spelt. Sometimes you have to write out the correct spelling or underline either those correctly or incorrectly spelt. It is important that you pay attention to the instructions otherwise you may make the error of, for example, underlining the correct spellings when you were asked to underline the incorrect ones. Try the following examples:

Example 1. Underline the *correct* spellings.

Wedesday	Febuary	indecate	butiful
sincerely	foreign	sataday	archetec
immediate	equiped	merchandise	juvenille
deliverys	mashinery	shampoo	responcibility

Example 2. Where the spelling is wrong write the correct spelling in the space alongside.

author	....	balence	....
beeutify	....	corelate	....
desease	....	foremost	....
holiday	....	occasion	....

Example 3. Locate the incorrectly spelt words among the group of seven words that make up a question, look up the number of the incorrect words on the list (all the words on the list are correctly spelt) and enter the numbers in the answer box. Your answers do not have to be in numerical order. One of the answers has been given.

List

1. among	11. hasten	21. warranty
2. balance	12. hypocrisy	22. writing
3. calendar	13. imprecise	23. yield
4. creative	14. knuckle	24. yourself
5. delayed	15. league	25. zeal
6. disturb	16. numerous	
7. emphasis	17. plasticity	
8. equality	18. receive	
9. forgery	19. secretary	
10. generous	20. vacuum	

1.

calendar	hypocrisy
recieve	balance
amoung	vacum
yourself	

Answer

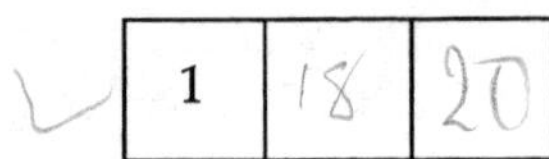

2.

zeal	warrantie
delaiyded	generous
plasticity	hasten
secretery	

Answer

4. Tests of Logical Thinking

Sometimes you have to follow instructions in this type of test or you may be expected to work out relationships and then make a prediction.

A. Following instructions

There are a wide number of variations on this type of test. The instructions you have to follow often include the alphabet and numbers. These types of question may or may not be multiple choice. Here is a useful tip: with this sort of question it helps if you take one clause at a time. Try these examples:

Example 1

If Wednesday comes before Friday and May comes before December, place the second letter of the alphabet in the answer box. Otherwise place the first letter of the word Wednesday in the answer box.

Answer

Example 2

Divide the largest figure with the smallest and then add the result to the second figure from the left.

4	6	12	9	3	8	7

A	B	C	D	E
8	7	10	1	6

Answer

B. Relationships between numbers and statements

In this sort of question you have to say what you think logically fits the gap or will come next. Sometimes you are expected to identify which is the odd one out from a collection of numbers, words or shapes. Try these examples:

Example 1. What number fits the gap?

7	11	...	19	23

Answer

Example 2. Which is the odd one out?

(a) The Isle of Wight
(b) Anglesey
(c) Skye
(d) Stoke on Trent

Answer

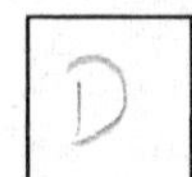

Example 3. Which is the odd one out?

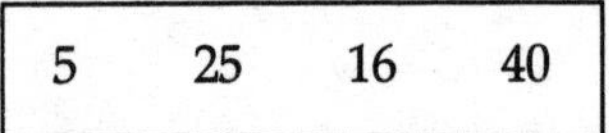

Answer

Example 4. Which is the odd one out?

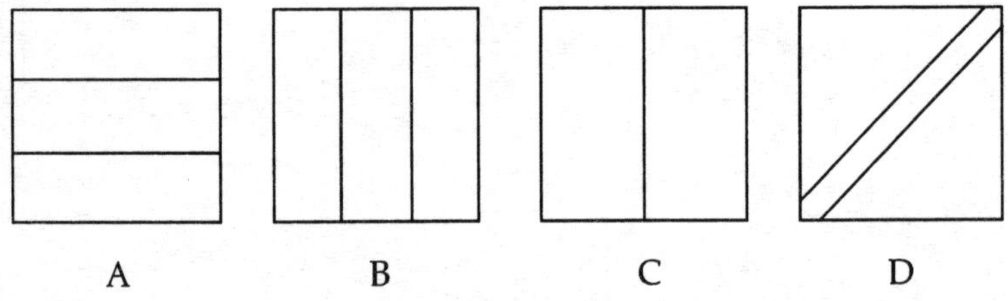

Answer

5. Numerical Tests

Most numeracy tests require you to complete a variety of sums that will test your command of the four rules: addition, subtraction, multiplication and division. Try the following examples without using a calculator. Do not worry if you get stuck; there are lots more practice examples given later in the book.

A. The four rules

1. Add

   980054
   60273
   ______ Answer

2. Subtract

   607389
   236571
   ______ Answer

3. Add twice then subtract the smaller answer from the greater.

   5 + 17 + 5 =
   12 + 6 + 11 =
   ______ Answer

4. Divide

   $12 \overline{)4920}$ Answer

5. Multiply

   50746
   26
   ______ Answer

6. Multiply twice then divide the lesser answer into the greater.

   $6 \times 40 =$
   $4 \times 3 =$
   Answer

Make sure that your answers are in the correct place.

B. Practical numerical problems

Some companies are concerned that you can not only carry out basic mathematical calculations but also apply them in practical situations. To test this ability they use the following kinds of question.

Example 1

If a first class stamp costs 26 pence how much would 50 first class stamps cost?

Answer

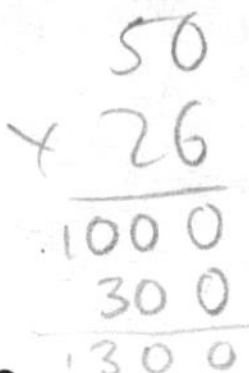

Example 2

If the balance of petty cash is £93.70 before you were instructed to purchase stationery to the value of £20.18 what would be the new balance?

Answer

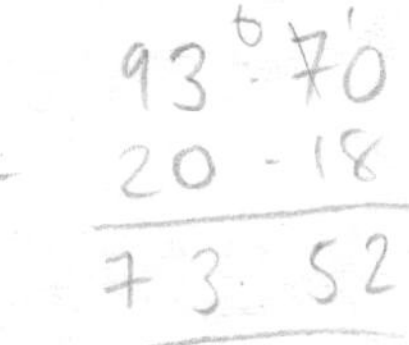

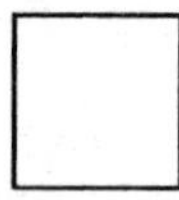

Example 3

Fourteen people attended the annual office party and the cost was £350. How much is that per head?

Answer

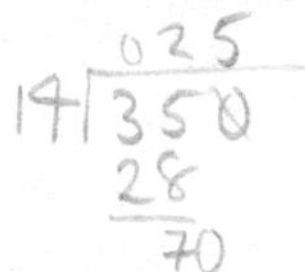

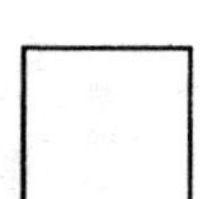

Example 4

The office photocopier service contract is charged at 1.4 pence each copy. How much would be charged for 1500 copies?

Answer

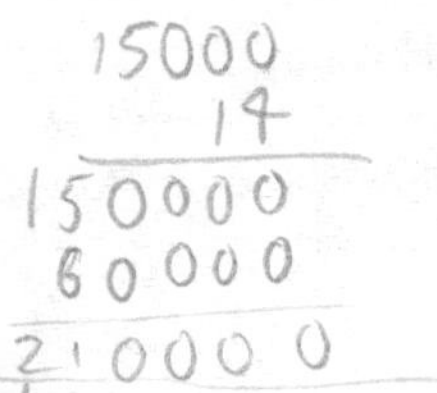

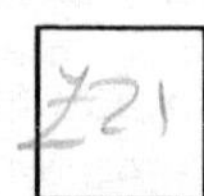

C. Estimating/approximating

This type of test sets out to measure your ability to approximate the answer to calculations. Usually, this type of test is multiple choice and the amount of time allowed does not allow you to work out answers exactly. Try these examples:

Example 1

48 + 55 =

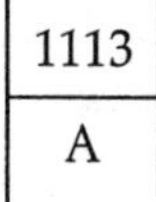
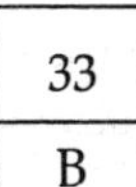

1113	33	203	103	93
A	B	C	D	E

Answer

Example 2

12 × 9 =

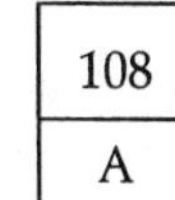

108	78	128	1108
A	B	C	D

Answer

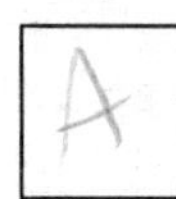

D. Percentages and fractions

In addition to the four rules discussed and illustrated above, some tests also examine your command of fractions and percentages. The questions may take any of the forms so far covered. For example:

Example 1

$\frac{1}{2} + \frac{2}{3} + \frac{1}{4} =$

Example 2

$\frac{1}{4} + 2\frac{1}{3} + \frac{1}{2} =$

$3\frac{1}{12}$	$2\frac{1}{12}$	$1\frac{1}{12}$	$\frac{1}{12}$
A	B	C	D

Answer

Example 3

Your employer asked if you would work overtime at time and a half. Your normal rate of pay was £4.50 a hour. How much an hour would you earn while working overtime?

Answer

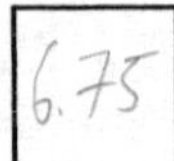

Example 4

The cost of a new fax machine was £640 without value added tax. If the tax was 17.5% how much would the total cost of the fax machine be?

Answer

Example 5

What is 24% of £380?

Answer

Example 6

Estimate 65% of 350

508	227.5	58	1208
A	B	C	D

Answer

6. Tests of Clerical and Computing Skills

These tests attempt to measure a candidate's aptitude for computing and clerical work. You may have to sit them as part of a battery of tests that could include verbal and numerical tests as described above. They include following coded instructions, interpreting flow diagrams, suggesting the appropriate sequence of events, and checking that data has been accurately inputted. Try the following examples:

A. Flow diagrams

Flow diagrams are used to represent a sequence of events, their interconnections and outcomes. Study the flow diagram below; it represents the opening of a computer file. Use it to answer the question.

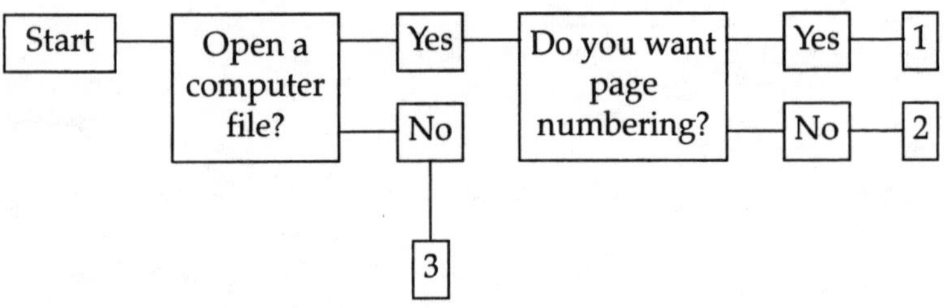

Question

A user wishes to open a file without page numbering. Which outcomes does the user require: 1, 2 or 3?

Answer

B. Sequencing

These are tests in which you have to put a set of items or instructions into a defined order. Sometimes the items are everyday things like going to work or they may be particular to computing. Try the following:

Write what you believe is the correct order for these events in the answer box.

Word processing

Switch off the power	Input the data	Save the file	Start the computer	Open the file
1	2	3	4	5

Answer

C. Coded instructions

This type of question involves sets of rules which you have to interpret and then apply. Try the following example:

Below are a set of codes and their meanings. You have to use this information to answer the series of questions.

Code

To open a file	OF	To check the spelling in a file	SP
To copy a file	CF	To save a file	SF
To leave the program	ESC		
To delete a file	DF		

Questions

What is the code:

1. To open a file? Answer ☐

2. To delete a file and leave the program Answer ☐

3. To open a file, check the spelling and save the file? Answer ☐

D. Checking computer data

In these tests you are provided with both the original information and a computer printout. You have to check to see whether the data has been accurately inputted on to the computer files.

Example:

In this example you have to check line by line the computer data against the original. If you find any discrepancies mark the answer box with the letter N; if the line has been accurately copied mark the box with the letter Y.

The answer to the first example has been given below.

Original Information

1	Land Sales Ltd	9 Lancia Place	Lancaster Gate	ES2 5HJ
2	Fox Associates	143 West Side	Ealing	5HJ 6TT
3	Colliers Building	68 Cambridge Street	Queens Way	3DD 5TG
4	Top Creation	11 George Road	Plaistow	9NN 4RF
5	Victoria Packing Systems	34a Major Street	Great Hardwood	2DE 6VC
6	Municipal Supplies	22 Warehouse Road	Small Heath	8MN 6AS
7	Berton Hotel	78 Baker Street	Uxbridge	12FD 5TT
8	Save Finance	53 Church Yard Close	Sherman	7FC 4DX
9	Longsdale Ltd	2 Burton Street	Hackney	E5 2CD
10	Western Electronics	10 Resister Road	East Ham	E6 4RF
11	New Technologies	13 Fourth Avenue	Manor Park	E12 5NT
12	Net Surfing Cafe	20 Cyber Street	Compton	CB13 7FG
13	Super Robotics Plc	145 Wells Street	High Grove	HG8 2WL
14	Info Tech Ltd	1 New Lane	Hertfordshire	NW3 2SA
15	Printer Printers	2 Print Street	Printington	PT5 2PR

1	Land Scales Ltd	N
	9 Lanca Place	N
	Lancaster Gate	Y
	ES2 5HJ	Y

2	Fox Associates	☐
	143 West Side	☐
	Ealing	☐
	5HJ 6TT	☐

3	Collers Building	☐
	68 Cambridge Street	☐
	Queeens Way	☐
	3DD 5TG	☐

4	Top Creation	☐
	11 Gorge Road	☐
	Plaistow	☐
	9NN 4RF	☐

5	Victoria Pack Systems	☐
	34a Major Street	☐
	Great Harwood	☐
	2DE 6VC	☐

6	Municipal Supplies	☐
	22 Warehouse Road	☐
	Small Health	☐
	8MN 6AS	☐

7

Barton Hotel
78 Baker Street
Uxbidge
12DD 5TT

8

Save Finances
53 Church Yard Close
Sherman
7FC 4DX

9

Longsdale LTD
2 Burton Street
Hackney
E5 2CD

10

Western Electronic
10 Resister Rood
EastHam
E9 4RF

11

New Technology
13 Forth Avenue
Manor Park
E12 5NT

12	Net Surfing Cafe	
	20 Cyber Street	
	Compton	
	CB13 7FG	

13	Super Robotics PLc	
	145 Well Street	
	High Grove	
	HG8 2WL	

14	Info Tech Ltd	
	1 New Lane	
	Hertfordshire	
	NW3 25A	

15	Printers Printers	
	2 Print Street	
	Printington	
	PTS 2PR	

When you check your answers, go over the exercises that you got wrong again and see if you can work out your mistake.

5 Practice Material

This chapter consists of practice exercises relevant to some of the most common types of test currently used for selection purposes. The exercises are divided into three categories: verbal, numerical and clerical.

Time limits have been suggested for some of the exercises and answers can be found on pages 130–152. When you check your answers try not to see simply how many questions you got right; instead, go back over the questions and try to work out why you went wrong. That way you are learning.

Verbal Tests

1. The Same Meaning or the Opposite

Underline the word that has the same meaning and circle the word that has the opposite meaning as the word on the *left*. For example:

elastic	brittle	hidden	stretchy	action

Try these:

store	stockpile	sieve	tent	waste
wrong	nail	catch	mistaken	right
question	answer	misery	describe	enquire
measure	artery	volume	guess-work	gauge
problem	absent	concave	solution	obstacle
obscure	objective	transparent	conceal	
synthetic	man-made	music	thought	natural

vertical	horizontal	upright	topmost	
repair	impair	neglect	recondition	test
strengthen	lengthen	purify	augment	weaken

If you do not know the answers to any of these examples look them up in a dictionary. You could also try a Thesaurus which lists synonyms (words that mean the same). Once you have finished the exercise, why not make up some examples of your own?

Your grasp of synonyms and opposites may be tested in a variety of ways. Here are some examples of the way these type of question are worded. Try them and make up examples of your own.

You have to underline the correct answer.

1. Car is to motor boat as bike is to:

pedalo	rowing boat	sailing boat	submarine

Now make up an example of this type of question yourself:

__________ is to __________ as __________ is to:

2. Skill means the same as:

weak	ability	inept	cunning

Make up an example of this type of question:

__________ means the same as:

__________ __________ __________ __________

3. Which of the following means fight?

brute	burn	brawn	brawl

Make an example:

Which of the following means __________?

__________ __________ __________ __________

4. Hard is to soft as stone is to:

rock	water	mud	marble

Make up an example of this kind of question:

________ is to __________ as __________ is to:

5. Long means the opposite of:

high	low	short	wide

Make up an example yourself:

________ means the opposite of:

__________ __________ __________ __________

2. Sound Alike/Look Alike Words

Some words have different meanings but sound identical or very similar, for example:

site (place) and sight (view)

Other words again have different meanings but look similar, for example:

dairy (milking shed) and diary (memoir)

Words that sound or look like other words are often used in verbal selection tests and it is surprising how often the same examples come up. It may help if you are clear over the difference between the meaning of some common examples.

Use a dictionary if necessary to be clear about the difference in meaning between the pairs of words below. Then make up sentences that demonstrate the difference. For example, in the case of site and sight:

Sentence 1. The site is over on the left.

Sentence 2. It rained all the way and by the time they arrived they were quite a sight.

Now write a sentence for the word 'cite' which also sounds like site and sight.

Sentence 3. ____

____

Be sure you understand the difference in meaning of these sound alike/look alike words.

Exercise 1

morning mourning
be bee
whether weather
course cause
specific pacific
boar bore
effect affect
stationary stationery
practice practise

ascent assent
here hear
right write
except accept
meet meat
allowed aloud
council counsel
there their
waist waste

principal principle
edition addition
piece peace
brake break
advise advice
excess access
though through threw
for fore four

You have 2 minutes in which to place the correct pairs of words from the above lists into the gaps in the sentences below.

1. We . . . . down on him.
   The . . . . was in the cage next to the elephant.
2. You need to be more . . . . in the use of your words.
   We looked out across the . . . . ocean.
3. He went this . . . .
   She is in . . . .
4. It was the . . . . of the matter.
   We had to do it, after all she was the . . . .
5. I was up to my . . . . in it.
   It seemed so wrong that there was so much . . . .
6. . . . . I waited for over half an hour.
   The sound of some words gives an indication of . . . . meaning.

Exercise 2

You are presented with a number of sentences. In each sentence you will find two or more words placed in brackets. Your task is to choose one word that best completes the sentence and write it in the space provided.

1. All the guests (knew, new) each other at the party.

   ANS . . . .

2. There was (to, too, two) much traffic on the motorway.

   ANS . . . .

3. In a South American country the (guerrillas, gorillas) were on the verge of gaining control of the capital city.

   ANS . . . .

4. The (rap, wrap) on the door caused John to awaken from his dream.

   ANS . . . .

5. There were only a (few, phew) television sets left in the shop.

   ANS . . . .

6. Louise was asked to collect the (draft, draught) from the bank on her way to work.

   ANS . . . .

7. It was all (quiet, quite) on the Western Front.

   ANS . . . .

8. All the (writes, rights, rites) were performed by the local priest.

   ANS . . . .

9. That building was built in the 17th century and was originally an (arms, alms) house.

   ANS . . . .

10. In the old days, water pipes were made from (led, lead).

    ANS . . led . . . . ✗

11. The gale force wind was (effecting, affecting) the television reception.

    ANS . . affecting

12. They found it difficult to decide (whether, weather) to go to Spain or to France for the holiday.

    ANS . . whether

13. The lorry driver (accepted, excepted) that it was his fault.

    ANS . . accepted

14. It was a great (feet, feat) that the climbers achieved.

    ANS . . . feat . .

15. She placed the bottles over (there, their, they're) on the table.

    ANS . . there . .

16. To quote is to (cite, site, sight).

    ANS . . cite . . .

17. The computer should not be switched (of, off) until the disk has been removed.

    ANS . . off . . . . . .

18. The surgery was full of (patients, patience) waiting to see the doctor.

    ANS . . patients

19. The postman put the letters (through, threw) the letterbox.

    ANS . . through

20. At the interview Jane was asked to take a (sit, seat).

    ANS . . . .

21. Children should be seen and not (heard, herd).

    ANS . . . .

22. Kathy said her voice felt very (horse, hoarse).

    ANS . . . .

23. The postman always brings the (male, mail) at 8.30.

    ANS . . . .

24. The (scene, seen) from the hill top was magnificent.

    ANS . . . .

25. Everyone went to the party (accept, except) James.

    ANS . . . .

26. When the phone rang, Jane and Chris were on (there, their, they're) way out to the shops.

    ANS . . . .

3. Choosing the Right Word

In many verbal tests you have to choose a word from a number of options which you believe completes the sentence correctly. Try the following examples:

Instructions

You have to choose a word from the box that in your opinion correctly completes the sentence, then write that word in the space.

1. I left the car over ____________.

there, their

2. I could not have ____________ another thing.

eaten, ate

3. ____________ the post arrived yet?

has, have

4. It looks ____________ it is going to rain.

like, as, as though

5. ____________ was it her fault.

or, nor

6. I knew ____________ it was going to happen.

that, what

7. We __________ talking when he interrupted.

were, was

8. My sister and __________ went to see our grandmother.

me, I

4. Timed Exercise – Choosing the Right Word

Over the page you will find 10 questions. Before you turn over, set a clock or watch to allow yourself 5 minutes to complete them.

Instructions

Choose from the suggested answers the words which you believe correctly complete the sentence and write them in the space provided.

It could be a question of either spelling, grammar or meaning.

Do not turn the page to begin the timed exercise until you are ready.

1. They all ________ that she was ________.

knew, leave, new, gnu, leaving, leafing

2. ________ should ________ seen them.

ewe, you, had, have

3. She is a very ________ young ________.

abel, able, women, woman

4. I do hope the ________ will be ________.

weather, whether, fine, fined

5. We ________ ________ this morning.

flew, flu, flue, accross, across

6. We must ________ to ________.

agreement, agree, agreed, differ, difer

7. My eyes are __________ from looking at the __________ screen.

tied, tyred, tired, colour, colore

8. The results are given in the __________ and __________ below.

colum, column, rows, roes, rouse

9. Can this __________ be __________ on our computer?

program, programme, uses, used

10. The __________ __________ called and asked if you would phone back.

centre, centaur, manger, manager

END OF EXERCISE

5. Choosing the Right Sentence

Sometimes verbal tests require you to choose a sentence rather than a particular word. This type of test can examine your command of punctuation as well as grammar, spelling and syntax (meaning). Try the following examples:

1.

A. I thought that their was a problem with the laser printer?
B. I thought that there was a problem with the laser printer.
C. I through that their was a problem with the laser printer.
D. I through that they're was a problem with the laser printer.

Answer

2.

A. The matter will be given immediate attention.
B. The matter will be given mediate attention.
C. The matter will be given mediate attension.

Answer

3.

A. In response to the interest you have expressed in our product I enclose the relevant information, order form and price list.
B. In responce to the interest you have expressed in our product I enclose, the relevant information, order form and price list.
C. In responce to the interest you have expressed in our product I enclose the relevant information order form and price list.

Answer

4.

A. The most common form of dismissal involves the termination of a worker's contract with notice.
B. The most common form of dismissal involves the termination of a workers' contract with notice.
C. The most common form of dismissal involves the termination of a workers contract with notice.

Answer

5.

A. Childcare facilties have being made available.
B. Childcare facility have been made available.
C. Childcare facilities have been made available.
D. Childcare facilities has been made available.

Answer

Here is a useful tip: it helps if you not only look for the correct answer but also try to rule out some of the sentences by recognising them as incorrect.

Over the page are 10 further examples of this type of question. Check your watch and allow yourself 5 minutes to complete them.

Do not turn the page to begin the timed exercise until you are ready.

6. Timed Exercise – Choosing the Right Sentence

1.

A. There is the man whom represents the company.
B. There is the man which represents the company.
C. There is the man who represents the company.
D. There is the man what represents the company.

Answer

2.

A. Luckily the error was discovered before the end of the physical year.
B. Luckily the error was discovered before the end of the fiscal year.
C. Luckily the era was discovered before the end of the fiscal year.
D. Luckily the era was discovered before the end of the physical.

Answer

3.

A. In the enclosed envelop you will find the reciept.
B. In the enclosed envelope you will find the receipt.
C. In the enclosed envelope you will find the reciept.
D. In the enclosed envelop you will find the receipt.

Answer

4.

A. David said John is late.
B. 'David said' John is late.
C. David said, 'John is late'.
D. David, 'said John', is late.

Answer

5.

A. The committee sat much later than expected.
B. The comittee sat much latter than expected.
C. The committee sat much later than accept.
D. The committe sat much later than expected.

Answer

6.

A. I like Fridays and I hate Mondays.
B. I like Fridays both I hate Mondays.
C. I like Fridays nor I hate Mondays.
D. I like Fridays but I hate Mondays.

Answer

7.

A. There really is an access of filing to be done.
B. There really is an excess of fileing to be done.

C. There really is an access of fileing to be done.
D. There really is an excess of filing to be done.

Answer

8.

A. Try not to allow your expenditure to exceed what you urn.
B. Try not to allow your expenditure to accede what you earn.
C. Try not to allow your expenditure to exceed what you earn.
D. Try not to allow your expenditure to excess what you earn.

Answer

9.

A. Colin was born on the 19th August, at King Street Hospital Manchester, his father was at work.
B. Colin was born on the 19th August, at king street hospital Manchester his father was at work.
C. Colin was Born on the 19th August at King Street Hospital manchester his Father was at Work.
D. Colin was born on the 19th August at King Street hospital Manchester his father was at work.
E. Colin was born on the 19th August, at King Street Hospital, Manchester; his father was at work.

Answer

Manchester; his father was at work.

10.

A. The delivery of stationary is two days late.
B. The delivery of stationery is too days late.
C. The delivery of stationary is to days late.
D. The delivery of stationery is two days late.

END OF EXERCISE

You might find it useful to go back over these exercises at your own pace.

7. Plural words

You are given a word for which you have to find the correct plural spelling from a list on the right-hand side. Now try this and see how you get on.

1. Interview
   A. Interviewees
   B. Interviewers
   C. Interviews
   D. Interviewes
   E. None of these

2. Vacancy
   A. Vacancys
   B. Vacancyes
   C. Vacancise
   D. Vacancies
   E. None of these

3. Shelf
   A. Shelfs
   B. Shelves
   C. Shelfes
   D. Shelvses
   E. None of these

4. Match
   A. Matchees
   B. Matches
   C. Matcheses
   D. Matchses

5. Business
   - A. Business
   - B. Businesses
   - C. Businessis
   - D. Businessies
   - E. None of these

6. Monkey
   - A. Monkees
   - B. Monkeyes
   - C. Monkeies
   - D. Monkies
   - E. None of these

7. Family
   - A. Familys
   - B. Familyes
   - C. Familese
   - D. Families
   - E. None of these

8. Message
   - A. Messages
   - B. Messagess
   - C. Messagies
   - D. Messagees
   - E. None of these

9. Donkey
   - A. Donkeyes
   - B. Donkeyies
   - C. Donkeies
   - D. Donkies
   - E. None of these

10. Photocopy
    - A. Photocopis
    - B. Photocopyes
    - C. Photocopyis
    - D. Photocopies
    - E. None of these

11. Ability
    - A. Abilitys
    - B. Abilityes
    - C. Abilites
    - D. Abilities
    - E. None of these

12. Capacity
   A. Capacites
   B. Capacitis
   C. Capaciteis
   D. Capacities
   E. None of these

13. Adjective
   A. Adjectives
   B. Adjectivies
   C. Adjectivees
   D. Adjectivyes
   E. None of these

14. Allegory
   A. Allegores
   B. Allegories
   C. Allegoryes
   D. Allegoryies
   E. None of these

15. Ambiguity
   A. Ambiguities
   B. Ambiguityes
   C. Ambiguitys
   D. Ambiguites
   E. None of these

16. Antique
   A. Antiquies
   B. Antiques
   C. Antiqueys
   D. Antiqueis
   E. None of these

17. Customer
   A. Customeres
   B. Customerse
   C. Customers
   D. Customeries
   E. None of these

18. Disguise
   A. Disguises
   B. Disguisees
   C. Disguisess
   D. Disguisies
   E. None of these

19. Euphemism
   A. Euphemismes
   B. Euphemisms
   C. Euphemismse
   D. Euphemismies
   E. None of these

20. Hoof
   A. Hoofs
   B. Hoovs
   C. Hoofes
   D. Hooves
   E. None of these

21. Guarantee
   A. Guaranteies
   B. Guaranteses
   C. Guarantees
   D. Guaranteis
   E. None of these

22. Machine
   A. Machinies
   B. Machines
   C. Machinees
   D. Machins
   E. None of these

23. Negative
   A. Negatives
   B. Negativeis
   C. Negativies
   D. Negativees
   E. None of these

24. Personality
   A. Personalities
   B. Personalites
   C. Personalitees
   D. Personalityes
   E. None of these

25. Platitude
   A. Platituds
   B. Platitudes
   C. Platitudus
   D. Platitudas
   E. None of these

26. Psychologist
    A. Psychologistes
    B. Psychologists
    C. Psychologisties
    D. Psychologistees
    E. None of these

27. Rhyme
    A. Rhymies
    B. Rhymes
    C. Rhymses
    D. Rhymeies
    E. None of these

28. Sequence
    A. Sequences
    B. Sequencees
    C. Sequenceies
    D. Sequencies
    E. None of these

29. Taxi
    A. Taxies
    B. Taxis
    C. Taxise
    D. Taxes
    E. None of these

30. Roof
    A. Roofs
    B. Roovs
    C. Roofes
    D. Rooves
    E. None of these

31. Sense
    A. Senseces
    B. Sencees
    C. Sensies
    D. Sensees
    E. None of these

32. Thief
    A. Thiefes
    B. Thieves
    C. Thievse
    D. Thiefves
    E. None of these

33. Statesman
A. Statesmans
B. Statesmens
C. Statesmen
D. Statesman
E. None of these

34. Technology
A. Technologyes
B. Technologies
C. Technologys
D. Technologees
E. None of these

35. Language
A. Languagies
B. Languagees
C. Languagese
D. Language's
E. None of these

8. Spelling

Below is a list of 75 words, spelt correctly and in alphabetical order.

On the following pages you will find groups of nine words. In each group there may be up to four spelling errors. Your task is to find the word or words that are incorrectly spelt. Once you have found these words you then have to locate them in the list below in which spellings are correct and write the number in the answer box.

For your assistance an example has been given. Study the example and then complete the eight questions.

1. Abbreviate
2. Absolute
3. Accountant
4. Alternative
5. Autumn
6. Beautiful
7. Beneficial
8. Billiards
9. Boutique
10. Broadcast
11. Brutus
12. Bustle
13. Canada
14. Carburettor
15. Category
16. Caterpillar
17. Centrifugal
18. Complementary
19. Definite
20. Defeatism
21. Designer
22. Develop
23. Devotee
24. Diffidence
25. Diplomatically
26. Earring
27. Economically
28. Egalitarian
29. Eligible
30. Emperor
31. Equilibrium
32. Exaggerate
33. Failure
34. February
35. Fiction
36. Flotation
37. Formula
38. Functionalism
39. Gallon
40. Geometric
41. Gesture
42. Goggle
43. Gradual
44. Graphology
45. Handkerchief
46. Harbour
47. Hexagon
48. Homogenous
49. Hospital
50. Humiliate
51. Illustrate
52. Impatient
52. Inadmissible
54. Incompatible
55. Inflammable
56. Jostle
57. Junction
58. Ladder
59. Language
60. Laughter
61. Leadership
62. Magistrate
63. Manage
64. Marginal
65. Mercury
66. Middle
67. Minimum
68. Monetary
69. Napkin
70. Neighbour
71. Nightingale
72. Northern
73. Nucleus
74. Numerous
75. Nurture

For example:

Brodcast	Fiction	Leadership
Handkerchief	Formular	Earing
Hospital	Napkin	Hexagon

10	37
26	

In this example there are only three errors, but as explained there can be up to four.

1.

Minnimum	Gradual	Centriugal
Deffinite	Northern	Jostle
Exaggerate	Defeatism	Homegenous

2.

Absolute	Ecconomically	Benefitial
Brutus	Napkin	Fiction
Ladder	Goggle	Mercury

3.

Language	Boutique	Failure
Gallon	Gestture	Devotee
Impatient	Febuary	Nurture

4.

Busle	Caterpillar	Complementary
Desiner	Humiliate	Marginal
Harbor	Manage	Canada

☐ ☐

☐ ☐

5.

Laughter	Graphology	Flotation
Geometric	Catagory	Deffinite
Hospital	Nightingale	Middle

☐ ☐

☐ ☐

6.

Egaletarian	Josle	Develop
Homogenous	Nucleaus	Accountant
Canada	Illustrate	Inflamable

☐ ☐

☐ ☐

7.

Autum	Harbour	Neighbour
Defaetism	Emparor	Ladder
Billiards	Gallon	Numerious

8.

Failure	Minnimum	Nightingale
Devalop	Humiliate	Northern
Mercurey	Carburettor	Difidence

9. Timed spelling

Over the page are 10 further examples of this type of question. Check your watch and allow yourself *10* minutes to complete them.

Do not turn the page to begin the timed exercise until you are ready.

1. Alternate
2. Amalgamation
3. Anaesthesia
4. Analogous
5. Appeasement
6. Arbitrary
7. Assessor
8. Broach
9. Bullion
10. Ceremonious
11. Chancellor
12. Dismantle
13. Diversity
14. Exhaustion
15. Expedient
16. Flippant
17. Frustrate
18. Genealogy
19. Guillotine
20. Hereditable
21. Humility
22. Indentation
23. Invention
24. Journal
25. Justify
26. Knife
27. Kitchen
28. Lagging
29. Latitude
30. League
31. Magazine
32. Mansion
33. Minister
34. Nitrate
35. Nominate
36. Numeration
37. Nutritious
38. Oath
39. Obsession
40. Omission
41. Orchestra
42. Pantomime
43. Parochial
44. Penicillin
45. Petition
46. Pneumonia
47. Pygmy
48. Quadrangle
49. Quicken
50. Quinine
51. Quintillion
52. Radiate
53. Rampage
54. Rapture
55. Recital
56. Rendezvous
57. Ridiculous
58. Safeguard
59. Satellite
60. Scaffolding
61. Scientist
62. Scratch
63. Segregate
64. Solemnize
65. Tangible
66. Technician
67. Temporarily
68. Tongue
69. Undulate
70. Utility
71. Variety
72. Velvet
73. Warranty
74. Wealthiness
75. Xylophone

1.

Alternate	Broch	Petition
Neumonia	Pigme	Tongue
Rampage	League	Minister

☐ ☐

☐ ☐

2.

Flippant	Justify	Outh
Valwet	Asessor	Quicken
Safegard	Rapture	Invention

☐ ☐

☐ ☐

3.

Exhustion	Kitchen	Manshun
Nitrate	Recital	Justify
Bullion	Chansellor	Varity

☐ ☐

☐ ☐

4.

Amalgamation	Technician	Obsession
Geneology	Journul	Knife
Magazine	Humility	Radiate

☐ ☐

☐ ☐

5.

Zylophone
Pantomime
Ceremonious

Penicillin
Parocail
Anaesthesia

Orcastra
Utility
Omission

6.

Warranty
Divercity
Tanjible

League
Guillotine
Temporarily

Appesement
Scientist
Latitute

7.

Hereditable
Frustrate
Omission

Indentation
Dismantel
Rondevous

Resital
Arbitary
Nominate

8.

Ridiculuous
Segregate
Quinine

Scraach
Numeration
Satallite

Expedient
Petition
League

9.

Quadangle
Rapture
Alternate

Solemize
Obsesion
Undulate

Lagging
Nitrate
Warrantee

10.

Nutritious
Hereditable
Scaffolding

Rapchure
Indentation
Flippant

Welthiness
Latitude
Temprarily

END OF EXERCISE

10. Reading for Information

You are presented with some passages to read. A number of statements follow each passage. Your task is to say whether the statement is true or false. The statement can only be true if the information in the passage bears this out.

Example

The great fire of London started in Pudding Lane, near London Bridge, in the year 1666. It was probably the worst fire in the City's history.

1. The great fire of London took place in 1666.

   True or False (underline one of these)

When the American War of Independence started, the Americans had no regular army. But one was soon formed under the command of George Washington. However, this army was badly equipped and lacked proper training.

The war lasted for six years, from 1775 to 1781, and the Americans drew up the formal Declaration of Independence on 4th July 1776. This stated that the United States would be an independent republic.

1. The highly trained American army quickly won the war.

   True or False

2. The war lasted for six years and the declaration of independence was made shortly after the end of the war.

   True or False

3. The first regular American army was commanded by Washington.

   True or False

The brain begins to show signs of decline after a certain proportion of the nerve cells of which it is formed have died. As people get older they have fewer and fewer nerve cells, because once the cells have died they are not replaced.

By the time a person reaches the age of 75 as many as a quarter of the nerve cells may have died.

Although science has advanced a great deal and scientists today are better placed to study how our brain functions, there is still a great deal to discover.

4. By the time a person is in his mid-seventies he may have lost as many as 25% of his nerve cells.

   True or False

5. Scientists today are able to cure the dying nerve cells, because of the great advances made by science.

   True or False

6. The brain cells, like the skin cells, are able to multiply and that is why all the brain cells do not die out.

   True or False

The problem with the notion of technology is that there are various meanings of the term. It no longer has a precise and limited meaning, but rather a vague and expansive one.

The term is used to describe not only instruments and machines but also skills, methods and procedures, among other things.

Some commentators have argued that technology is a factor that determines key facets of organisations.

However, others have argued that there is no cause and effect relationship between adoption of the technologies and the structural and performance outcomes that may be associated with them.

7. Everyone agrees with the single definition of technology.

   True or False

8. When people talk about technology they are always referring to machines, such as computers.

   True or False

9. Some people have argued that technology is a determining factor in a number of key areas of an organisation.

   True or False

For more (and more difficult) examples of this type of question, see *How to Pass Graduate Recruitment Tests* (published by Kogan Page).

11. Alphabetical Order

The alphabet: A B C D E F G H I J K L M N O P Q R S T U V W X Y Z.

Arranging words – Example 1

Place the following words in the answer box in alphabetical order:

Gangster	Kidnap
Puff-adder	Sorrow
Acrobat	Orator
Heiress	Reptile

Answer box

1.	5.
2.	6.
3.	7.
4.	8.

Arranging words – Example 2

Now arrange the following into alphabetical order:

Faithful	Foliage
Fixer	Farmyard
Florida	Fabric
February	Feather

Answer box

1.	5.
2.	6.
3.	7.
4.	8.

Rearranging letters

1. Rearrange the letters in 'charity' into alphabetical order. Place your answer in the answer box.

Answer box

2. Rearrange the letters in 'liquor' into alphabetical order. Place your answer in the answer box.

]Answer box

3. Rearrange the letters in 'organic' into alphabetical order. Place your answer in the answer box.

Answer box

4. Rearrange the letters in 'Thames' into alphabetical order. Place your answer in the answer box.

Answer box

5. Take the letters that occur in 'Delphi' but not in 'delta' and write them in alphabetical order in the answer box.

Answer box

6. Take the letters that occur in 'kidney' but not in 'kilograms' and write them in alphabetical order in the answer box.

Answer box

7. Take the letters that occur in 'petrol' but not in 'Peru' and write them in alphabetical order in the answer box.

Answer box

8. Take the letters that occur in 'chamber' but not in 'chaise' and write them in alphabetical order in the answer box.

Answer box

Over the page you will find a timed exercise that requires knowledge of alphabetical order.

Before you turn over, set a clock or watch and allow yourself 3 minutes.

Instructions

Alongside each name write the file number under which the name should be placed.

The first two examples have been completed.

File numbers

1. A–Am	10. J–K
2. An–Az	11. L–M
3. B–Bs	12. N–O
4. Bt–Bz	13. P–Q
5. C–Ck	14. R
6. Cl–Cz	15. S
7. D–E	16. T
8. F–G	17. U–V
9. H–I	18. W–X, Y–Z

Name	File Number	Name	File Number
Young	18	Warner	_____
Bayard	3	Carrington	_____
Harvey	_____	Christie	_____
Fisher	_____	Tooling	_____
Skinner	_____	Arnold	_____
Bishop	_____	Hood	_____
Adler	_____	Dell	_____

12. Comparisons 1

1. Man is to boy as woman is to:

   A. Lady B. Girl C. Madam D. Lad

2. Food is to eat as water is to:

   A. Swallow B. Bathe C. Drink D. Shower

3. Man is to house as monkey is to:

   A. Tree B. Jungle C. Cave D. Nest

4. Car is to bicycle as aeroplane is to:

   A. Jet B. Sky C. Glider D. Flying

5. Ship is to sea as train is to:

   A. Station B. Platform C. Rail D. Journey

6. He is to him as she is to:

   A. She's B. Her C. Their D. Hers

7. Cotton is to thread as copper is to:

   A. Mesh B. Wire C. Electricity D. Insulation

8. Shoes are to feet as gloves are to:

   A. Fingers B. Hands C. Toes D. Arms

9. Hat is to head as sweater is to:

   A. Chest B. Torso C. Arms D. Back

10. Floppy disk is to computer as a suitcase is to:

    A. Teacher B. Traveler C. Technician D. Trainee

Comparisons 2

Now try the following and see how many you can do in two minutes.

1. Pen is to ink as pencil is to:

   A. Quill B. Lead C. Eraser D. Crayon

2. Black is to white as light is to:

   A. Lamp B. Bulb C. Dark D. Bright

3. A is to B as Y is to:

   A. Z B. Y C. X D. W

4. M is to P as G is to:

   A. H B. L C. J D. N

5. F is to L as R is to:

   A. X B. Y C. H D. G

6. Eraser is to pencil as snowpake is to:

   A. Chalk B. Pen C. Paintbrush D. Stencil

7. Story book is to read as exercise book is to:

   A. Study B. Doodle C. Write D. Draw

13. Odd-One-Out

	A	B	C	D	E
1.	A. Computer	B. Printer	C. Mouse	D. Keyboard	E. Monitor
2.	A. Hands	B. Feet	C. Fingers	D. Brain	E. Eyes
3.	A. See	B. Taste	C. Hear	D. Nose	E. Feel
4.	A. Wrist	B. Elbow	C. Finger	D. Thumb	E. Toe
5.	A. Dry	B. Arid	C. Parched	D. Desert	E. Swamp
6.	A. Horse	B. Camel	C. Pig	D. Oxen	E. Elephant
7.	A. Pen	B. Pencil	C. Quill	D. Chalk	E. Stencil
8.	A. Lion	B. Tiger	C. Leopard	D. Baboon	E. Cheetah
9.	A. Lantern	B. Lamp	C. Sun	D. Candle	E. Torch
10.	A. Lake	B. Pond	C. River	D. Reservoir	E. Pool
11.	A. Telephone	B. Television	C. Facsimile	D. Telex	E. E-mail
12.	A. Teacher	B. Trainer	C. Lecturer	D. Instructor	E. Examiner

14. Opposites

1. Down is the opposite of:

   A. Horizontal B. Up C. Fallen D. Crouching

2. Inflated is the opposite of:

   A. Blown-up B. Deflated C. Reflated D. Conflated

3. Append is the opposite of:

   A. Add B. Restore C. Remove D. Revert

4. Correct is the opposite of:

   A. Solution B. Error C. Right D. True

5. Enter is the opposite of:

   A. Come in B. Arrive C. Exit D. Welcome

6. Covert is the opposite of:

   A. Closed B. Open C. Divert D. Revert

7. Restore is the opposite of:

   A. Destroy B. Repair C. Reinstate D. Mend

8. Drunk is the opposite of:

   A. Tipsy B. Sober C. Intoxicated D. Incapable

9. Cool is the opposite of:

   A. Freeze B. Warm C. Boil D. Frozen

10. Vertical is the opposite of:

    A. Upright B. Erect C. Horizontal D. Upside-down

15. Similar Sounding Words But Different Spelling and Meanings

In this exercise you have to find a word which sounds the same as the word that you are given but is spelt differently.

Exercise 1

For example

full *fool*

1.	Sight	________	2.	Course	________
3.	Draft	________	4.	Broach	________
5.	New	________	6.	Dam	________
7.	Weather	________	8.	Due	________
9.	Mail	________	10.	Die	________
11.	Gale	________	12.	Sweet	________
13.	Write	________	14.	To	________
15.	Read	________	16.	Tail	________
17.	Bye	________	18.	One	________
19.	Wave	________	20.	For	________
21.	Need	________	22.	Flower	________
23.	Breach	________	24.	Sole	________
25.	Seen	________	26.	Hair	________
27.	Sun	________	28.	Heard	________
29.	Seem	________	30.	Heart	________

Exercise 2 See how many you can do in 5 minutes.

1.	Fate	________	2.	Hear	________
3.	Great	________	4.	Hole	________
5.	No	________	6.	Main	________
7.	Bored	________	8.	Ale	________
9.	Bold	________	10.	Night	________
11.	Bare	________	12.	Knit	________
13.	Brake	________	14.	Miner	________
15.	Bread	________	16.	Naval	________
17.	Sent	________	18.	None	________
19.	Meet	________	20.	Or	________
21.	Of	________	22.	Peace	________
23.	Peel	________	24.	Pair	________
25.	Peek	________	26.	Plate	________
27.	Pole	________	28.	Pull	________
29.	Pour	________	30.	Rain	________
31.	Pray	________	32.	Program	________
33.	Pearl	________	34.	Key	________
35.	Rest	________	36.	Rap	________
37.	Reek	________	38.	Ring	________
39.	Rye	________	40.	Shoe	________

16. Written Statements/Tests

Sometimes when you attend an interview you are asked to write a short statement, of at least 50 words, explaining why you want the job or what you think are the most important aspects of the work. A time limit is imposed.

You are usually told in advance that you will be asked to undertake such an exercise so you can prepare your statement beforehand.

If you know that you are going to have to write a statement, ask someone to help you prepare it. If you keep the sentences short your statement will be easier to read.

Make sure your statement is positive. Consider incorporating, in your own words, points about the work made in the advertisement or information sent to you by the organisation.

You should memorise your statement the night before. Read it aloud again and again, then write it out repeatedly. Keep learning your statement until you are able to write it without notes or prompting. Learn the spelling of any words of which you are unsure.

Try writing your statement in the time that you are allowed – usually 10 minutes – and make sure that your handwriting is neat and legible.

Numerical Tests

On pages 87–106 you will find practice examples which you can work through at your own pace and which become progressively harder. You will also find timed examples. We have tried to ensure that the severity of these timed examples is comparable to the types of question you would face in a real selection test.

If you can do the timed sums, or learn to do them, in the time suggested, you can have confidence in yourself because you are likely to do well in most types of numerical test.

Do not use a calculator except to check your answers. There is not space here to show you how to do these calculations. If you are unable to do some of them, ask a friend to show you. Alternatively, your local library will have books that demonstrate how to do these sums together with further practice examples.

Some tests set out to measure your skills in approximating the answer to calculations. Even if you do not have to face such a test, it is a useful skill to develop as it can lead to your being far quicker in many types of numerical test, and can also help to keep a check on calculations performed on a calculator.

To help you develop this skill we have provided you with estimating exercises for each of the four rules and for fractions and percentages.

Estimating is very useful in the case of multiple-choice numerical tests.

When you approximate do not work the sum out; instead, use your knowledge of the relationship between numbers to make an educated guess at the answer. Round up numbers to the nearest convenient figure and look at the suggested answers for the nearest to your estimate.

This section is divided into three parts: the first deals with the four rules, percentages and fractions; the second offers exercises in approximating; and the third consists of practical numerical problems.

1. The Four Rules, Percentages and Fractions

Addition

See if you can work these out within 5 minutes.

1. 2 + 1 =
2. 3 + 6 =
3. 4 + 3 =
4. 1 + 9 =
5. 10 + 1 =
6. 11 + 7 =
7. 16 + 8 =
8. 11 + 16 =
9. 69 + 0 =
10. 36 + 10 =
11. 0 + 0 =
12. 120 + 30 =
13. 1.1 + 1 =
14. 1.5 + 1.5 =
15. 10.5 + 10 =
16. 0.5 + 3.6 =
17. 10 + 10 + 20 =
18. 100 + 5 + 200 =
19. 1200 + 400 + 40 =
20. 67 + 50 + 19 =
21. 750 + 250 + 10 =
22. 0.5 + 3.6 + 0.5 =
23. 0.4 + 0.5 + 0.1 =
24. 375 + 50 + 55 =
25. 0.75 + 35 + 1.25 =
26. 120 + 60 + 13 =
27. 15 + 35 + 150 =
28. 0.65 + 1.35 + 5 =
29. 0.25 + 0.45 + 0.3 =
30. 1.4 + 2.4 + 2.4 =

Subtraction

Now work these out.

1. 8 – 3 =
2. 12 – 9 =
3. 16 – 0 =
4. 71 – 29 =
5. 15.5 – 13.5 =
6. 10.66 – 8.3 =
7. 9654 – 3247
8. 8435 – 3253
9. 76540 – 47450
10. 63904 – 42615
11. 398004 – 75205
12. 6700.19 – 986.11
13. 506.65 – 45.37
14. 3020.26 – 543.88
15. 7021.03 – 1264.43

Now try to work these out in 3 minutes.

16. 70053 30536
17. 50605.03 4317.06
18. 900.802 625.837

If you cannot get these right in the suggested time you need further practice.

Multiplication

Work these out.

Simple multiplication

1. 5863 × 5
2. 950 × 4
3. 1637 × 3
4. 2486 × 4
5. 369 × 7

Long multiplication

6. 5689 × 15
7. 5868 × 17
8. 66085 × 10
9. 2560919 × 205
10. 150897 × 350

Long multiplication with decimals

11. 60593 × 3.2
12. 963.40 × 24
13. 76003 × 96.05

Here is a useful tip: keep your calculation neat and the numbers aligned, otherwise you may add up the wrong columns.

Division

Work these out. Place your answers along the top of each sum.

Simple division

1.	2.	3.
$4\overline{)12}$	$12\overline{)72}$	$8\overline{)56}$
4.	**5.**	**6.**
$6\overline{)24}$	$5\overline{)950}$	$7\overline{)315}$

Long division (get help if you can't do these)

7.	8.	9.
$17\overline{)1105}$	$11\overline{)11220}$	$16\overline{)7632}$

Division with decimals

10.	11.	12.
$25\overline{)330}$	$12.2\overline{)140.3}$	$17\overline{)209.1}$

You have to practise a lot and know your tables before you become both quick and accurate at these exercises.

Division to time. You have 3 minutes.

1.	2.	3.
$27\overline{)6048}$	$12\overline{)126}$	$18.4\overline{)465.52}$

Percentages

Work these out.

1. 25% of 100 =
2. 30% of 70 =
3. 20% of 50 =
4. 90% of 25 =
5. 75% of 1000 =
6. 65% of 2560 =
7. ?% of 5500 = 3025
8. ?% of 7350 = 3454.50
9. 36% of ? = 243
10. 17% of ? = 14.79
11. ?% of 950 = 47.5
12. 3% of ? = 25.95
13. 6% of 66 =
14. If 6.8 is 8% what is 100%?
15. If 1.6 is 4% what is 100%?

Fractions

If you are applying for a technical job in telecommunications or engineering you may be asked to do fractions.

Work out the missing fraction or number.

1. $\frac{2}{2} = ?$ 2. $\frac{4}{1} = ?$ 3. $\frac{2}{4} = ?$

4. $\frac{30}{3} = ?$ 5. $\frac{50}{?} = 10$ 6. $\frac{?}{4} = 2$

Work these out.

7. $\frac{1}{2}$ of 28 =

8. $\frac{3}{4}$ of 20 =

9. $\frac{1}{3}$ of 60 =

10. $\frac{1}{4}$ of 100 =

If you cannot do these, ask for help.

Work these out.

11. $\frac{1}{4} + \frac{1}{3} + \frac{2}{6} =$

12. $1\frac{1}{2} + \frac{1}{6} + \frac{2}{3} =$

13. $6 \times \frac{3}{4} =$

14. $6\frac{1}{2} \times 5\frac{1}{4} =$

This is how hard these types of calculation are in real tests.

Try to do the next three examples in 3 minutes.

15. $1\frac{1}{2} + \frac{5}{6} + \frac{9}{12} =$

16. $\frac{5}{6}$ of 192 =

17. $\frac{45}{9} \times 5 =$

If you got all three right in the 3 minutes, you ought to do well in a numerical test containing this sort of question.

Don't give up if you cannot do these. If you have time get help or enrol on a numeracy course at your local college of further education or adult education institute.

2. Approximating

Rounding off numbers (1)

The purpose of this exercise is to help you make rough calculations quickly. This is particularly useful when you are presented with several answers and you have to choose one of them. By rounding off numbers and then doing the calculations you will have an answer that will be near enough to the correct answer.

First, we will ask you to round off to the nearest whole number. Later you will have the opportunity to do some calculations.

Now try the following.

Example: 2.89 is nearest to 3

1. 99.99 is nearest to . . . . . .
2. 9.9 is nearest to . . . . . .
3. 1.89 is nearest to . . . . . .
4. 9.19 is nearest to . . . . . .
5. 7.8 is nearest to . . . . . .
6. 499.67 is nearest to . . . . . .
7. 115.10 is nearest to . . . . . .
8. 5.8892 is nearest to . . . . . .
9. 3.12 is nearest to . . . . . .
10. 6.2113 is nearest to . . . . . .
11. 2.102 is nearest to . . . . . .
12. 8.421 is nearest to . . . . . .
13. 5.6110 is nearest to . . . . . .
14. 7.9876 is nearest to . . . . . .
15. 44.898 is nearest to . . . . . .

Rounding off numbers (2)

In this exercise you have to convert the figures to the nearest convenient sum.

Example:

95% of 487 would become 100% of 500
29% of 291 would become 30% of 300

1. 19% of 694......................
2. 87% of 55...............................
3. 52% of 59........................
4. 20% of 987.............................
5. 47% of 188......................
6. 18% of 94...............................
7. 192% of 106....................
8. 9% of 888................................
9. 52% of 805......................
10. 43% of 82...............................
11. 8.9% of 39.8....................
12. 4.99% of 47.989......................
13. 4.965% of 98.932...........
14. 119.5% of 999.659..................
15. 9.98% of 699...................

Rounding off numbers (3)

In this exercise you should first round off the numbers before making the calculations, giving your answers in nearest whole numbers.

Example:

Add	6.983	is nearest to	7
	3.896	is nearest to	4
	1.883	is nearest to	2
Answer			13

Now try the following. Remember we only need the nearest answer, not the exact one.

1.	Add	5.8892	2.	Add	449.67
		3.12			99.99
		6.2113			1.89

3. Subtract 9.9
   1.89

4. Subtract 499.67
   199.76

5. Multiply 99.68
   1.95

6. Multiply 6969.763
   1.996

7. Divide 6969.763 by 1.996 __________
8. Divide 7998.687 by 3.893 __________
9. What is 10% of 9.99? __________
10. What is 20% of 9.99? __________
11. 3.321 + 4.1 + 10.1 __________
12. 699.76 + 99.89 __________
13. 699.76 – 99.89 __________
14. 9.9% of 49.789 __________
15. 49.9% of 9.9 __________

Addition

In this exercise you should approximate the answers as quickly as you can and then choose an answer from the box.

1. 0.49 + 399 + 49 =
2. 3098 + 2056 + 1078 =
3. 749 + 249 =
4. 2258.3 + 4934.1 + 5.2 =
5. 14.78 + 20.096 + 16.04 + 50 =
6. 1.5 + 59 + 39 + 50.5 =
7. 0.5 + 4.5 + 0.5 + 500.5 =
8. 509 + 309 + 209 + 203 =
9. 5035 + 6035 + 4030 =
10. 1559 + 2539 + 3332 =

7430	1230	15100
7709	448.49	6232
150	506	998
7197.6	100.916	200.919

Subtraction

Estimate the following:

You will be able to identify the correct answers far more quickly if you estimate rather than work out the calculations fully, round up figures to convenient sums, and look for the exact answers among those suggested in the box.

1. 139 – 17 =	2. 759 – 732 =	3. 9.87 – 7.95 =
4. 2987 – 499 =	5. 13.07 – 2.85 =	6. 634 – 171 =
7. 6278 – 1483 =	8. 555 – 326 =	9. 9987 – 399.12 =
10. 99.45 – 25.60 =		

10.22	73.85	122
4795	27	1.92
463	9587.88	229
2488		

Multiplication

In this exercise you should approximate the answers as quickly as you can and then choose an answer from the box.

1. $59 \times 5 \times 5 =$
2. $78 \times 10 \times 19 =$
3. $2.5 \times 10 \times 5 =$
4. $55 \times 3 \times 10 =$
5. $500 \times 0.5 \times 10 =$
6. $55 \times 6 \times 0.5 =$
7. $100 \times 100 \times 1 =$
8. $200 \times 100 \times 1.5 =$
9. $100 \times 0.9999 =$
10. $100 \times 0.5 \times 0.999 =$

49.95	99.99	225
30000	335	10000
445	165	2500
1650	555	125
14820	1475	665

Division

Estimate the following and choose an answer from the box:

1. $3\overline{)24.6}$
2. $9\overline{)198}$
3. $596\overline{)1072.8}$
4. $4.5\overline{)495}$
5. $9.9\overline{)9801}$

110	990	8.2	22	1.8

Percentages

In this exercise you should approximate the answers as quickly as you can and then choose an answer from the box.

1. 10% of 500 =
2. 20% of 600 =
3. 33% of 999 =
4. 49% of 749 =
5. 5% of 5000 =
6. 29% of 695 =
7. 18% of 95.99 =
8. 16% of 450 =
9. 11% of 19000 =
10. 9% of 5000 =

250	450	645
2090	750	201.84
855	17.28	72
50	367.01	960
329.67	540	120

Fractions

Estimate the following and choose an answer from the box:

1. $\frac{1}{4}$ of 55 =

2. $\frac{1}{3}$ of 24 =

3. $\frac{2}{3}$ of 90 =

4. $\frac{1}{4}$ of 124 =

5. $\frac{1}{2} + \frac{1}{3} + 1\frac{1}{4}$ =

8	60	$2\frac{1}{12}$	$13\frac{3}{4}$	31

Mixed

In this exercise you should approximate the answers. You should do this by rounding off the numbers and then roughly calculating the answer. Once you have done this, pick the correct answer from the box.

Now do these 10 questions in 5 minutes.

1. 29 + 41 + 29

2. 99 – 19

3. 19% of 49

4. 9 × 18

5. 395 ÷ 9

6. 0.9 + 89.1 – 14.6

7. 37% of 385

8. 845 ÷ 12

9. $\begin{array}{r} 456 \\ 654 \\ +123 \\ \hline \end{array}$

10. $\begin{array}{r} 5678 \\ -\ 4567 \\ \hline \end{array}$

11. $\begin{array}{r} 456 \\ \times\ 12 \\ \hline \end{array}$

12. 20 = X% of 400
What is X?

55	20	195
68	111	1111
1233	70.41	142.45
75.4	43.88	162
9.31	80	99
5472	4527	5

3. Practical Numerical Problems

Work these out without the use of a calculator.

1. Twenty-seven people are asked to contribute 50 pence each towards the cost of a leaving present for a colleague but three decline; how much is collected?

   Answer

2. Your telephone bill comprises a standing charge of £7.93, £40.47 worth of calls and £7.26 of value added tax. What is the total?

   Answer

3. Nicky works flexi-time and is contracted to work a 35-hour week. For three weeks she has only worked 27½ hours a week. How many hours does she owe?

   Answer

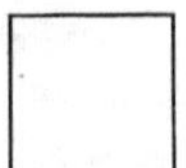

Work towards getting this sort of sum right consistently and quickly.

4. A large company employs 15% of the working population in a small town. The total population of the town is 70,000 of which 50% is the working population. How many people are employed by the company?

Answer

5. A shop sells washing machines for £150 plus VAT at 17.5%. What is the total price that customers would have to pay?

Answer

6. The same shop has a special offer on a video and television when bought together. The combined price is £650 inclusive, less a discount of 12%. What is the special offer price?

Answer

7. A clerical officer earns £12,000 gross per year. She is entitled to a tax-free personal allowance of £3000 and pays income tax at 25% on the balance. What is her net pay per year?

Answer

8. A senior clerical officer earns £15,000. What is the annual net pay, assuming all the other information is as above?

Answer

9. A businessman buys 500 pairs of shoes at a cost of £5000. He wants to make a 30% profit. What is the price he should charge for a pair of shoes?

Answer

10. A woman buys a television for £550, a CD player for £450, a computer for £850. She gets a 10% discount from the total price. How much has she paid?

Answer

If her two sons contribute two-thirds of the total cost, what would be the woman's share of the cost?

Answer

11. If Michael has £50, Chris has 50% more than Michael, and Betty has only half as much as Chris, how much money does Betty have?

Answer

12. An employer has 60 people working for her and she wants to give a 15% bonus to all her staff. How much would each staff member receive if the total weekly wage bill is normally £15,000?

Answer

13. How much would each staff member receive if the bonus is reduced to 10%?

Answer

14. Claire earns £430.60 per week but £86.12 income tax and £43.60 National Insurance contributions are deducted. How much net pay does she receive?

Answer

Over the page you will find three more of these exercises to be done against time. You have 3 minutes.

Do not turn the page to begin the timed exercise until you are ready.

1. A restaurant bill totals £42.80 and is to be divided between four people. How much has each person to pay?

Answer

2. How much value added tax, charged at 17.5%, would be added to a pre-tax total of £88?

Answer

3. If a two-kilowatt electric fire costs 10.7 pence an hour to run, how much would it cost to operate a one-kilowatt fire for sixteen hours?

Answer

Your speed and accuracy at this sort of calculation will greatly improve with practice.

Foreign currency exchange rates

Here is a table of different foreign currencies. The values shown are equal to one pound sterling. For example: £1 = 10 francs.

French Francs	10
Dutch Gilders	5
Italian Lira	2500
German Marks	3
US Dollars	1.80
Indian Rupees	65

Using the above exchange rates calculate the following:

1. A customer wishes to purchase 390 German Marks. How many pounds will she have to pay?

   A. 390 B. 230 C. 190 D. 130 E. None of these

2. How many Indian Rupees can you get for £350?

   A. 600 B. 6500 C. 7500 D. 5650 E. None of these

3. How many pounds would you get for 126 Francs?

   A. 10 B. 15 C. 12.60 D. 10.50 E. None of these

4. What are 500 Gilders worth in German Marks?

   A. 100 B. 200 C. 300 D. 400 E. None of these

5. Convert 250,000 Lira into Indian Rupees. How many Rupees is that?

   A. 1250 B. 6500 C. 2500 D. 100 E. None of these

6. If you bought 90 US Dollars and 600 French Francs, how many pounds would you require?

   A. 250 B. 150 C. 125 D. 110 E. None of these

French Francs	10
Dutch Gilders	5
Italian Lira	2500
German Marks	3
US Dollars	1.80
Indian Rupees	65

7. A tourist has £500 with which he intends to purchase some foreign currencies. He decides to buy Francs for 25% of the pounds, Marks for a further 25% and with the remaining 50% of the pounds he decides to buy Italian Lira. What are the different amounts of currencies that the tourist will get?

	A.	B.	C.	D.	E.
Francs	1600	1300	1400	1250	None
Marks	375	475	275	375	of
Lira	625,000	635,000	625,000	625,000	these

8. A woman returning from a holiday finds that she still has some foreign money left. She has 300 Dutch Gilders, 500 US Dollars and 50 Francs in change which she is not able to exchange. What is the total amount of pounds she will get?

   A. 377.78 B. 337.78 C. 327.78 D. 347.78 E. None of these

9. A French tourist wishes to buy 850 Dollars. How many Francs will that cost him?

   A. 7566.67 B. 5056.67 C. 4722.22 D. 6666.67 E. None of these

10. An American brings 7200 Dollars with her to London and wants to exchange them for pounds. How many pounds would she get after paying a 10% commission charge?

    A. 2600 B. 3600 C. 4600 D. 5600 E. None of these

Clerical Tests

These exercises will help in your preparation for the types of selection test that companies use to assess your suitability for clerical work and work with computers.

1. Coded instructions

These involve sets of rules or tables of information that you interpret and then apply to a series of situations or refer to in order to answer a series of questions.

Exercise 1

Establish from the table the answers to the questions.

Time	What happened	Where we were
9 am	the telephone rang	out shopping
12.00	the post arrived	watching the news on TV
1 pm	I paid the milk bill	on the door step
2 pm	did the washing	down the launderette
4 pm	cooked dinner	in the kitchen

Questions

1. Where was I at 2 pm? ______
2. What was I doing at 12.00? ______
3. What time was it when I was watching TV? ______
4. What was I doing while on the door step? ______
5. When did the post arrive? ______
6. What time did the phone ring? ______

Exercise 2

In this exercise you are required to translate the English sentences into the code equivalents by referring to the dictionary.

Dictionary

call	ranch
Fido	Tratma
dog	lippgai
is	nitco
black	modod
the	udyne

Example:

Call Fido = Ranch Tratma

Questions

1. The dog is black. ______________________
2. Fido is the dog. ______________________
3. Call the black dog. ______________________

Now translate these coded sentences into English.

1. Tratma udyne lippgai. ______________________
2. Nitco Tratma modod?______________________
3. Nitco udyne lippgai Tratma?______________________

Exercise 3: Computerised accounts system for a building society

Codes

Current account	C
Share account	S
Fixed account	F
Loan account	L

The code for the type of account is followed by an account number and a code indicating whether the account is in credit or overdrawn.

Account in credit	OC
Account overdrawn	OD

Example:

A fixed account number 00210 in credit = F00210OC

Answer the following questions by selecting one of the suggested answers A, B, C or D. Indicate your answer by writing either A, B, C or D in the answer box.

Questions

1. A current account number 3679830 in credit.

A. S367830OC
B. L3679830OC
C. C33679830OC
D. C3679830OC

Answer

2. A share account number 2213730 overdrawn.

A. L2213730OC
B. S2213730OD
C. F2213730OC
D. C2213730OD

Answer

☐

3. A loan account number 087231 in credit.

A. C087231OD
B. S087231OC
C. L087231OD
D. L087231OC

Answer

☐

Over the page is a timed coded instructions exercise. Allow yourself 5 minutes to answer the five questions.

Do not turn the page until you are ready to do the timed exercise.

A computerised till in a shop

> If payment is made by credit card it is coded CT.
>
> Payment by cheque is coded CHQ.
>
> For cash the code is CS.
>
> If the amount is less than £50 the letter U follows the code.
>
> If the amount is over £50 the letter O follows the code.
>
> For all furniture items the number 1 follows the letter U or O.
>
> Other goods are numbered 2.

Answer the following questions by selecting one of the suggested answers. Indicate your answer by writing A, B, C or D in the answer box.

Example:

A man buys a suit for £150 and pays by credit card.

A. CTO1
B. CTU1
C. CTO2
D. CTU2

Answer

1. A couple buy a dining table for £99 and pay cash.

A. CS
B. CHQ
C. CS2
D. CSO1

Answer

2. A woman buys a shirt for £25 and pays by cheque.

A. CHQ
B. CGQ1
C. CHQ2
D. CHQU2

Answer

3. A man buys a chair for £49.99 and pays by credit card.

A. CTO1
B. CTU1
C. CTO2
D. CSU2

Answer

4. A bed is bought for £250 cash.

A. CTQ1
B. CTU1
C. CTO2
D. CSO1

Answer

5. Someone writes a cheque out to the value of £199.95 in payment of a colour TV.

A. CTU2
B. CSO1
C. CQHU2
D. CHQO2

Answer

More examples of this type of question can be found in the Kogan Page title, *How to Pass Computer Selection Tests.*

END OF EXERCISE

2. Flow Diagrams

These exercises require you to interpret the information presented and use it to answer the questions.

Exercise 1: A catalogue order procedure

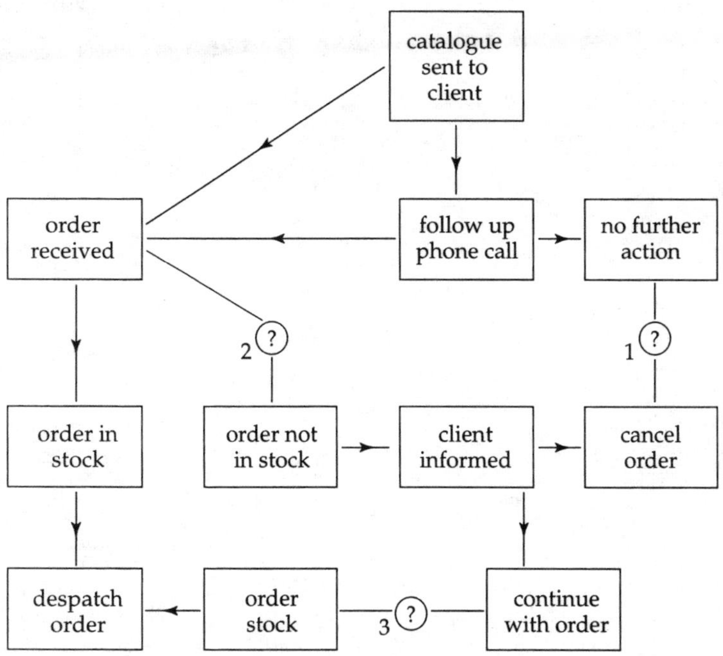

Study the flow diagram and decide which way the arrows ought to be drawn at points 1, 2 and 3. Indicate your answer by drawing arrows in the answer boxes provided.

1.

Answer

2.

Answer

3.

Answer

Exercise 2: A finance department's invoice system

Interpret the flow diagram and answer the questions.

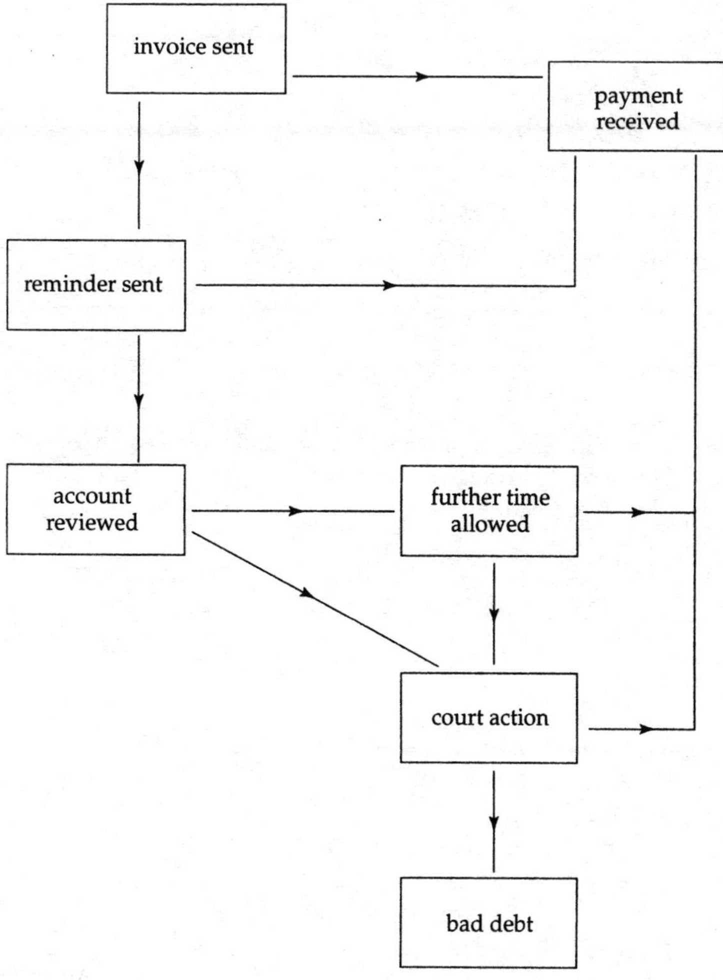

1. It was decided at the account review to give a customer extra time to pay but that time has now passed without result. What action should the accounts manager initiate?

Answer:

____

2. No payment has been received for an invoice. What action should be taken?

Answer:

____

3. If a reminder is sent after 30 days and the account review held after a further 30 days, what is the minimum period before court action is instigated?

Answer:

____

Over the page is a timed flow diagram exercise. Allow yourself 5 minutes to answer the five questions.

Do not turn the page until you are ready to do the timed exercise.

The recruitment process of a leading employer

You have 5 minutes in which to study the flow diagram and answer the questions.

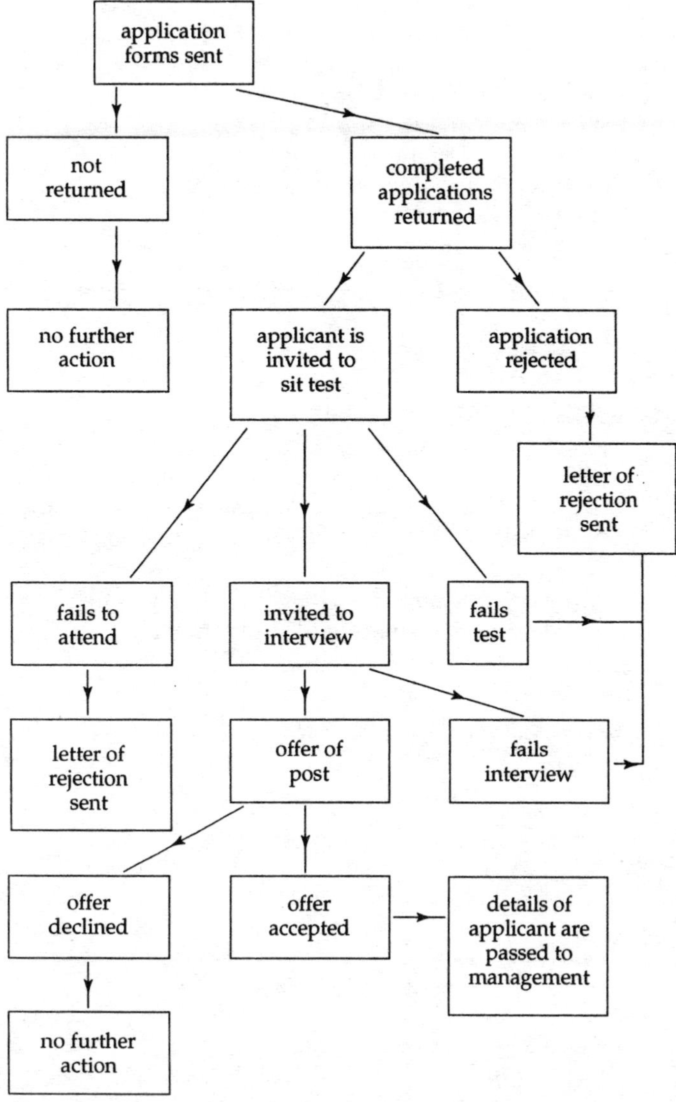

Indicate what the personnel officer should do if:

1. Someone fails to attend for interview.

Answer:

___

2. A candidate fails to return an application form.

Answer:

___

3. A candidate is successful at interview.

Answer:

___

4. A candidate submits a successful application form.

Answer:

___

5. A candidate accepts the offer of a post.

Answer:

___

END OF EXERCISE

3. Checking

In this exercise you are presented with a list of company names. On the left is the original list and on the right is a retyped version. Your task is to check the retyped version for any errors by comparing it with the original list on the left. Put brackets around the retyped version if there is an error.

Exercise 1

This exercise aims to assess your skills in checking speedily and accurately. Now complete this task in 3 minutes.

Paine Chocolates	Pain Chocolates
Pall Mall Dispensing	Pall Mall Dispensing
Lodge Insurance Brokers	Lodge Insurence Brokers
Lodder Est Agts	LOdder Est Agts
Mill Hill Dry Clnrs	Mill Hill Dry Clnrs
Kahn Printers	Kahn Printers
Italian Piano Co	Italian Piano Co
Hoxtex Restaurants	Hoxtex Restaurant
Apollo Bed and Breakfast	Apollo Bedand Breakfast
Holloway Carpenters	Holloway Carpenters
Archway Halal Meat	Archway Hala Meat
Hookway Jewellers	Hookway Jewellers
Hi-tec School of Motoring	Hi-tec School of Motoring
Totland Hire Centre	Totland Hire Center
George's Recruitment	Georges Recruitment
West End Consultants	West End Consultants
Court Cars	Court cars
House of Lighting	Hourse of Lighting
Woxton Water Works	Woxton Water Works
Castletown Restaurants	Castletown Recruitments
Hardwood Doors Group Ltd	Hardwood Doors Group LTD
Mike's Do It Yourself Centre	Mike's Do It Yourself Centre
MITAKA Publishing House	MITAKA Publsihing House
Sunchung Takeaway	Sanchung Takeaway
Move Motorcycle Hire	Move Motorcyycle Hire

Portman Car and Van Rental	Portman Carr and Van Rental
Heitman and Son Accountants	Heitman and son Accountance
Ace Consulting Engineers	Ace Consulting Engineers
Hot Tandoori House	Hot Tundoori House
Safe Security Ltd	Safe security Ltd

Exercise 2

Original	*Copy*
ABC123	ABC123
ACCB/123/321	ACCB/123/321
CENTIMETRES/CUBIC	CENTEMETRES/CUBIC
GUMPTION	GUMPTION
MEASURES/CAPACITY	MAESURES/CAPACITY
987654321/123456789	987654321/123456789
987/123/654/456:	987/123/654/456
GERMANIUM-72.59	GERMANUM-72.59
MOLYBDENUM-95.94	MOLYBDENUM-95.94
NICKEL-58.71	NICKLE-58.71
ZIRCONIUM-91.22	ZIRCONIUM-91.22
PHOSPHORUS-30.9738	PHOSPHOROS-30.9738
MILLILITRES-36966	MILLILITERS-36966
MANGANESE-54.9380	MANGANESE-54.9380
DECAGRAMMES-15432	DECAGRAMMS-15432
KILOGRAMME-2205	KILOGRAMMES-2205
ANTIMONY-121.75	ANTIMONY-121.75
HYDROGEN-1.0080(H)	HYDROGIN-1.0080(H)
CHROMIUM-51.996	CHROMUIM-51.996
MINNESOTA STATE	MINNISOTA STATE
ZEDEKIAH	ZEDEKIAH
WYOMING/ CHEYENNE	WYCOMING/ CHEYENNE
TENNESSEE/NASHVILLE	TENESSEE/NASHVILLE
ZOROASTER	ZOROASTER
PENNSYLVANIA/ H'BURG	PENNCYLVANIA/ H'BURG

WHISTLER	WHISLER
VERSAILLES	VERSAILES
VERRUCOSE	VERRUCOSE
UNHALLOWED	UNIHALLOWED
TREACHEROUS	TREACHEROUS
TREASURY	TREASUERY
SPARE-PART	SPAIRE-PART
ROUSSEAU	RUOSSEAU
EQUIVALENTS	EQIUVALENTS
FLOUNCE	FLUONCE
HARDENBERG	HARDENBERG

Exercise 3

Original	*Copy*
123/456/789/AC	123/456/789/AC
987/654/321/CA	987/654/321/CA
32323/452/CIC	32332/452/CIC
ACEG/818/658	ACEG/818/658
BDFH/4653/12	BDFH)4653/12
ZED/678/TLT/010	ZED/678/TLT/010
WORLD/VIEW/83	WORLD/VEIW/83
ZEBEDEE/F/JJ	ZEBFDEE/F/JJ
YETI/SNOW/MAN	YETI/SNOW/MAN
ORI/GIN/AL/212	ORI/GIN/AL/212
ADVERTISEMENT	ADVERITISEMENT
PERSONNEL/DEPT	PERSENNEL/DEPT
COM/PUT/ER/SYS/TEM	COM/PUT/ER/SyS/TEM
00/11/22/345/678	00/11/22/345/678
3456/0987/4321/32	3456/0987/4321/32
RO/AD/RU/NN/ER/234	RO/AD/RV/NN/ER/234
GAL/2001/200001/00	GAL/2001/20001/00
ISBN 0-561-15163-0	ISBN 0-561-15163-0
1010101/02020/300	1010101/02020/300
DATA-100/303/404/50	DATA/100/303/404/50

4. Following Coded Instructions (2)

To enter the computer, type	LOG/SYS
To use the word processing package, type	WP
To use the database package, type	DB
To use the spreadsheets package, type	SPS
To open a new file, type	OF/NAME
To open and edit an old file, type	EF/NAME
To delete a file, type	DF/NAME

Example:

To enter the computer and edit an old database file
Answer: LOG/SYS/DB/EF/NAME

Now try these.

Which code should be used for the following?

1. To enter the computer

   [1] SYS/LOG
   [2] EF/NAME/LOG/SYS
   [3] LOG/SYS
   [4] ON/COM/PU/TER
   [5] None of these

2. To delete a file from the database (assume you have already entered the computer)

   [1] DF/NAMEDB
   [2] DB/DF/NAME
   [3] DF/NAME/DB
   [4] DF/NAME/SPS/WP/DB
   [5] None of these

3. To enter the computer and create a new file on the word processor

   [1] OF/NAME/WP
   [2] OF/NAME/LOG/WP
   [3] LOG/WP/NAME/OF

[4] LOG/SYS/WP/OF/NAME
[5] None of these

4. To edit a spreadsheet file by entering the computer first

[1] ED/SPS/LOG/SYS
[2] EF/NAME/SPS/LOG/SYS
[3] LOG/SYS/EF/SPS/NAME
[4] LOG/SYS/SPS/OF/NAME
[5] None of these

5. To delete a file from the word processing package

[1] WP/EF/NAME/WP
[2] DF/NAME/WP
[3] WP/OF/NAME/
[4] DF/LOG/NAME
[5] None of these

6. To enter the computer and use the spreadsheets program

[1] LOG/SYS/USE
[2] LOG/SYS/SPS
[3] USE/SPS/COM/PUT/ER
[4] LOG/SPS/NAME
[5] None of these

7. To use the database by logging on to the system

[1] DB/LOG/SYS
[2] LOG/DB/ON/TO/SYS
[3] LOG/SYS/SPS
[4] LOG/SYS/DB
[5] None of these

8. To use the word processor to create a file once you have entered the computer

[1] WP/NAME/LOG
[2] LOG/WP/NAME
[3] LOG/WP/OF
[4] LOG/WP/NAME/OF
[5] None of these

5. Following Coded Instructions (3)

Checking databases

To enter the computer, type	LOG/SYS
To check database one, type	DBO
To check database two, type	DBT
To check database three, type	DBT/R
To delete a file from database, type	ND/followed by the code of the appropriate database
To create a file in the database, type	CF/followed by the database code

Which code should be used for the following?

1. To delete a file from database three (assume you have already entered the computer)

   [1] DBT/R
   [2] ND/LOG/DBT/R
   [3] ND/DBT/R
   [4] ND/DBO
   [5] None of these

2. To check database two (assume you have already entered the computer)

   [1] DBT
   [2] DBO
   [3] DBT/R
   [4] DBO/T/R
   [5] None of these

3. To enter the computer and check database one

   [1] DBO
   [2] LOG/SYS/DBO
   [3] LOG/SYS/DBT/R
   [4] DBT/R/O
   [5] None of these

4. To create a file in database two (assume you have already entered the computer)

   [1] LOG/SYS/CF/DBT
   [2] CF/DBO/T
   [3] CF/DBT
   [4] ND/DBT
   [5] None of these

5. To enter the computer and create a file in database three

   [1] CF/DBT/R
   [2] CF/DBT
   [3] ND/DBT/R
   [4] ND/DBT
   [5] None of these

6. To enter the computer and delete a file in database one

   [1] ND/DBO
   [2] LOG/SYS/ND/DBO
   [3] LOG/SYS/ND/DBT
   [4] LOG/SYS/ND/DBT/R
   [5] None of these

7. To enter the computer

   [1] LOG/SYS/DBO
   [2] LOG/SYS
   [3] LOG/ON/SYS
   [4] LOG/ON/DU/DE
   [5] None of these

8. To create a file in database two and then delete a file in database one (assume you have already entered the computer)

   [1] CF/DBO & CF/DBT
   [2] CF/DBT & CF/DBO
   [3] CF/DBT & ND/DBT
   [4] CF/DBT & ND/DBO
   [5] None of these

9. To enter the computer and check database three and then create a file in database two

   [1] LOG/SYS/DBT/R & CF/DBO
   [2] LOG/SYS/DBT/R & CF/DBT
   [3] LOG/SYS/DBT/R & CF/DBT/R
   [4] DBT/R & CF/DBT
   [5] None of these

10. To check database one, then create a file in database two and finally delete a file in database three (assume you have already logged on)

   [1] DBO & CF/DBT & ND/DBT/R
   [2] CF/DBO & DBO & ND/DBT/R
   [3] DBO & ND/DBT & CF/DBT/R
   [4] DBO/DBO/CF/DBT/RO/NG
   [5] None of these

6. Sequencing

In this exercise you have to put a list of events in a logical order.

Under each list of events there are a number of boxes in which you are to put the numbers of the events in their logical order.

Example: Creating a file in a word processor

1. Load program 2. Switch on computer
3. Type 4. Switch off computer 5. Save file

2	1	3	5	4

Now try these:

A. Going to work

1. Get on train 2. Get up 3. Go to platform
4. Get off train 5. Arrive at other end 6. Leave home
7. Get to station

B. Changing a wheel of a car

1. Put on spare wheel 2. Undo the bolts
3. Remove old wheel 4. Tighten bolts

C. Using a cash dispenser machine

1. Input amount of money required
2. Type in correct number
3. Remove card and money
4. Insert card

D. Borrowing a book from a library

1. Take the book to the librarian
2. Locate the appropriate book case
3. Note the index code
4. Locate the appropriate section of the library
5. Consult the book location index
6. Locate the book

E. Solving a problem

1. Apply the solution. 2. Identify the problem
3. Select the best solution
4. Suggest as many solutions as possible

F. Constructing a valid argument 1

1. Conclusion: Mary is a European
2. Germans are also Europeans
3. Mary is a German

G. Constructing a valid argument 2

1. Conclusion: Peter is not a European
2. Peter says he is an American subject
3. If he said he is American that means he cannot be European
4. Is Peter European?

H. Tom is a tall person but he is not taller than Jeff. Tom is taller than both George and Ray. Jeff is shorter than Chris. Write the first letter of the tallest person's name.

I. Raheel's father is called Naseem. Naseem has a brother called Khalid. The two brothers' father has a daughter, Gazala, who is older than Khalid but younger than Naseem. What is the relationship between Raheel and Gazala?

J. A car is being driven due North. After five miles it turns 180 degrees. Write the first letter of the direction in which the car is now travelling.

Further examples of this type of question can be found in the Kogan Page titles, *How to Pass Verbal Reasoning Tests, How to Pass the Civil Service Qualifying Tests* and *How to Pass Computer Selection Tests.*

6 Answers

Chapter 4: Some of the Most Common Types of Test

1. Verbal Tests That Measure Comprehension (page 20)

A. Swapping words

First example 'test' and 'hard'
Second example 'limit' and 'virtually'

B. Finding missing words

B

C. Locating words that mean the same or the opposite

First example C
Second example B

2. Tests of Grammar and Punctuation (page 32)

A. Choosing from a number of sentences

First example (c)
Second example (a)

B. Choosing from pairs of words

First example D
Second example D

3. Spelling Tests (page 25)

Example 1
You should have underlined:
sincerely, foreign, immediate, merchandise, shampoo

Example 2
You should have written out the following words:
balance, beautify, correlate, disease

Example 3
Question 1 1, 18, 20
Question 2 21, 5, 19

4. Tests of Logical Thinking (page 27)

A. Following instructions

Example 1 B
Example 2 C

B. Relationships between numbers and statements

Example 1 15
Example 2 (d) Stoke on Trent (all the others are islands)
Example 3 16
Example 4 C

5. Numerical Tests (page 30)

A. The four rules

1. 1040327
2. 370818
3. 2
4. 410
5. 1319396
6. 20

B. Practical numerical problems

Example 1 £13
Example 2 £73.52
Example 3 £25
Example 4 £21

C. Estimating/approximating

Example 1 D
Example 2 A

D. Percentages and fractions

Example 1 $1\frac{5}{12}$

Example 2 A
Example 3 £6.75
Example 4 £752
Example 5 £91.20
Example 6 B

6. Tests of Clerical and Computing Skills (page 36)

A. Flow diagrams

2

B. Sequencing

4, 5, 2, 3, 1

C. Coded instructions

1. OF
2. DFESC
3. OFSPSF

D. Checking computer data

1	Land Scales Ltd	N	9 Lanca Place	N	Lancaster Gate	Y	ES2 5HJ	Y
2	Fox Associates	Y	143 West Side	Y	Ealing	Y	5HJ 6TT	Y
3	Collers Building	N	68 Cambridge Street	Y	Queeens Way	N	3DD 5TG	Y
4	Top Creation	Y	11 Gorge Road	N	Plaistow	Y	9NN 4RF	Y
5	Victoria Pack Systems	N	34a Major Street	Y	Great Harwood	N	2DE 6VC	Y
6	Municipal Supplies	Y	22 Warehouse Road	Y	Small Health	N	8MN 6AS	Y
7	Barton Hotel	N	78 Baker Street	Y	Uxbrige	N	12DD 5TT	N
8	Save Finances	N	53 Church Yard Close	Y	Sherman	Y	7FC 4DX	Y
9	Longsdale LTD	N	2 Burton Street	Y	Hackney	Y	E5 2CD	Y
10	Western Electronic	N	10 Resister Rood	N	EastHam	N	E9 4RF	N
11	New Technology	N	13 Forth Avenue	N	Manor Park	Y	E12 5NT	Y
12	Net Surfing Cafe	Y	20 Cyber Street	Y	Compton	Y	CB13 7FG	Y
13	Super Robotics PLc	N	145 Well Street	N	High Grove	Y	HG8 2WL	Y
14	Info Tech Ltd	Y	1 New Lane	Y	Hertfordshire	Y	NW3 25A	N
15	Printers Printers	N	2 Print Street	Y	Printington	Y	PTS 2PR	N

Chapter 5: Practice Material

Verbal tests (pages 43–85)

1. The same meaning or the opposite (page 43)

	Opposites	*Same*
store	waste	stockpile
wrong	right	mistaken
question	answer	enquire
measure	guess-work	gauge
problem	solution	obstacle
obscure	transparent	conceal
synthetic	natural	man-made
vertical	horizontal	upright
repair	neglect	recondition
strengthen	weaken	augment

1. pedalo
2. ability
3. brawl
4. mud
5. short

2. Sound alike/look alike words (page 46)

Exercise 1

1. bore, boar
2. specific, Pacific
3. morning, mourning
4. principle, principal
5. waist, waste
6. there, their

Exercise 2

1. knew	14. feat
2. too	15. there
3. guerrillas	16. cite
4. rap	17. off

5. few
6. draft
7. quiet
8. rites
9. alms
10. lead
11. affecting
12. whether
13. accepted
18. patients
19. through
20. seat
21. heard
22. hoarse
23. mail
24. scene
25. except
26. their

3. Choosing the right word (page 50)

1. there
2. eaten
3. has
4. as though
5. nor
6. that
7. were
8. I

4. Timed exercise – choosing the right word (page 52)

1. knew	leaving
2. you	have
3. able	woman
4. weather	fine
5. flew	across
6. agree	differ
7. tired	colour
8. column	rows
9. program	used
10. centre	manager

5. Choosing the right sentence (page 54)

1. B
2. A
3. A
4. A
5. C

6. Timed exercise – choosing the right sentence (page 57)

1. C
2. B
3. B
4. C
5. A
6. D
7. D
8. C
9. E
10. D

7. Plural words (page 60)

1. C.
2. D.
3. B.
4. B.
5. B.
6. E.
7. D.
8. A.
9. E.
10. D.
11. D.
12. D.
13. A.
14. B.
15. A.

16. B.
17. C.
18. A.
19. B.
20. D.
21. C.
22. B.
23. A.
24. A.
25. B.
26. B.
27. B.
28. A.
29. B.
30. A.
31. E.
32. B.
33. C.
34. B.
35. E.

8. *Spelling (page 65)*

1.	67	17	19	48
2.	27	7		
3.	41	34		
4.	12	21	46	
5.	15	19		
6.	28	56	73	55
7.	5	20	30	74
8.	67	22	65	24

9. *Timed spelling (page 69)*

1.	8	46	47	
2.	38	72	7	58
3.	14	32	11	71
4.	18	24		
5.	75	41	43	

6.	5	13	29	65
7.	55	12	6	56
8.	57	62	59	
9.	48	64	39	73
10.	54	74	67	

10. Reading for information (page 74)

1. False
2. False
3. True
4. True
5. False
6. False
7. False
8. False
9. True

11. Alphabetical order (page 76)

Arranging words – Example 1
1. Acrobat
2. Gangster
3. Heiress
4. Kidnap
5. Orator
6. Puff-adder
7. Reptile
8. Sorrow

Arranging words – Example 2
1. Fabric
2. Faithful
3. Farmyard
4. Feather
5. February
6. Fixer
7. Florida
8. Foliage

Rearranging letters

1. achirty
2. iloqru
3. acginor
4. aehmst
5. hip
6. deny
7. lot
8. bmr

Timed exercise

Name	*File Number*	*Name*	*File Number*
Young	18	Warner	18
Bayard	3	Carrington	5
Harvey	9	Christie	5
Fisher	8	Tooling	16
Skinner	15	Arnold	2
Bishop	3	Hood	9
Adler	1	Dell	7

12. *Answers to Comparisons 1* (page 80)

1. B 2. C 3. A 4. C 5. C 6. B 7. B 8. B
9. B 10. B

Answers to Comparisons 2 (page 81)

1. B 2. C 3. A 4. A 5. A 6. B 7. C

13. *Answers to Odd-One-Out* (page 82)

1. A 2. D 3. D 4. E 5. E 6. C 7. E 8. D
9. C 10. C 11. A 12. E

14. *Answers to Opposites* (page 83)

1. B 2. B 3. C 4. B 5. C 6. B 7. A 8. B
9. B 10. C

15. Answers to similar sounding words (page 84)

Exercise 1

1. cite/site
2. coarse
3. draught
4. brooch
5. knew
6. damn
7. whether
8. dew
9. male
10. dye
11. gail/gayle
12. suite
13. right/wright
14. too/two
15. red
16. tale
17. buy/by
18. won
19. waive
20. four/fore
21. knead
22. flour
23. breech
24. soul
25. scene
26. hare
27. son
28. herd
29. seam
30. hart

Exercise 2

1. fete
2. here
3. grate
4. whole
5. know
6. mane
7. board
8. ail
9. bald
10. knight
11. bear
12. nit
13. break
14. minor
15. bred
16. navel
17. scent
18. nun
19. meat
20. oar
21. off
22. piece
23. peal
24. pear
25. peak
26. plait
27. poll
28. pool
29. pore
30. reign/rein
31. prey
32. programme
33. purl
34. quay
35. wrest
36. wrap
37. wreak
38. wring
39. wry
40. shoo

Numerical Tests (pages 86–100)

1. *The four rules, percentages and fractions (page 87)*

Addition

1. 3	2. 9	3. 7	4. 10	5. 11
6. 18	7. 24	8. 27	9. 69	10. 46
11. 0	12. 150	13. 2.1	14. 3	15. 20.5
16. 4.1	17. 40	18. 305	19. 1640	20. 136
21. 1010	22. 4.6	23. 1	24. 480	25. 37
26. 193	27. 200	28. 7	29. 1	30. 6.2

Subtraction

1. 5
2. 3
3. 16
4. 42
5. 2
6. 2.36
7. 6407
8. 5182
9. 29090
10. 21289
11. 322799
12. 5714.08
13. 461.28
14. 2476.38
15. 5756.60
16. 39517
17. 46287.97
18. 274.965

Multiplication

1. 29315
2. 3800
3. 4911
4. 9944
5. 2583
6. 85335

7. 99756
8. 660850
9. 524988395
10. 52813950
11. 193897.60
12. 23121.60
13. 7300088.15

Division

1. 3
2. 6
3. 7
4. 4
5. 190
6. 45
7. 65
8. 1020
9. 477
10. 13.2
11. 11.5
12. 12.3

Timed division

1. 224
2. 10.5
3. 25.3

Percentages

1. 25
2. 21
3. 10
4. 22.5
5. 750
6. 1664
7. 55%
8. 47%
9. 675
10. 87
11. 5%

12. 865
13. 3.96
14. 85
15. 40

Fractions

1. 1
2. 4
3. $\frac{1}{2}$
4. 10
5. 5
6. 8
7. 14
8. 15
9. 20
10. 25
11. $\frac{11}{12}$
12. $2\frac{1}{3}$
13. $4\frac{1}{2}$
14. $34\frac{1}{8}$
15. $3\frac{1}{12}$
16. 160
17. 25

2. Approximating (pages 93–99)

Rounding off numbers (1)

1. 100
2. 10
3. 2
4. 9
5. 8
6. 500

7. 115
8. 6
9. 3
10. 6
11. 2
12. 8
13. 6
14. 8
15. 45

Rounding off numbers (2)

1. 20% of 700
2. 100% of 50
3. 50% of 60
4. 20% of 1000
5. 50% of 200
6. 20% of 100
7. 200% of 100
8. 10% of 900
9. 50% of 800
10. 40% of 80
11. 10% of 40
12. 5% of 50
13. 5% of 100
14. 120% of 1000
15. 10% of 700

Rounding off numbers (3)

1. 15
2. 552
3. 8
4. 300
5. 200
6. 14000
7. 3500
8. 2000
9. 1
10. 2
11. 17

12. 800
13. 600
14. 5
15. 5

Addition

1. 448.49
2. 6232
3. 998
4. 7197.6
5. 100.916
6. 150
7. 506
8. 1230
9. 15100
10. 7430

Subtraction

1. 122
2. 27
3. 1.92
4. 2488
5. 10.22
6. 463
7. 4795
8. 229
9. 9587.88
10. 73.85

Multiplication

1. 1475
2. 14820
3. 125
4. 1650
5. 2500
6. 165
7. 10000
8. 30000
9. 99.99
10. 49.95

Division

1. 8.2
2. 22
3. 1.8
4. 110
5. 990

Percentages

1. 50
2. 120
3. 329.67
4. 367.01
5. 250
6. 201.84
7. 17.28
8. 72
9. 2090
10. 450

Fractions

1. $13\frac{3}{4}$
2. 8
3. 60
4. 31
5. $2\frac{1}{12}$

Mixed

1. 99 2. 80 3. 9.31 4. 162 5. 43.88
6. 75.4 7. 142.45 8. 70.41 9. 1233 10. 1111
11. 5472 12. 5

3. *Practical numerical problems (pages 100–106)*

1. £12.00
2. £55.66
3. 22½ hours
4. 5250 people

5. £176.25
6. £572
7. £9750
8. £12,000
9. £13
10. (a) £1665
    (b) £555
11. £37.50
12. £37.50
13. £25
14. £300.88

Timed practical numerical problems

1. £10.70
2. £15.40
3. 85.6 pence

Foreign currency exchange rates

1. D (130)
2. E (None of these)
3. C (12.60)
4. C (300)
5. B (6500)
6. D (110)
7. D (1250, 375, 625,000)
8. B (337.78)
9. C (4722.22)
10. B (3600)

Clerical Tests (pages 107–112)

1. Coded instructions (page 107)

Exercise 1

1. Down the launderette
2. Watching the news on TV
3. 12.00
4. Paying the milk bill
5. 12.00
6. 9 am

Exercise 2

1. udyne	lippgai	nitco	modod
2. Tratma	nitco	udyne	lippgai
3. ranch	udyne	modod	lippgai

Into English
1. Fido the dog
2. is Fido black?
3. is the dog Fido?

Exercise 3
1. D
2. B
3. D

Timed coded instructions exercise
1. D
2. D
3. B
4. D
5. E

2. Flow diagrams (pages 113–118)

Exercise 1

1.

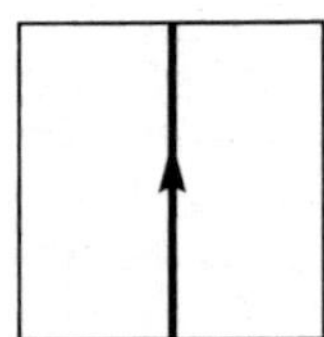

2.

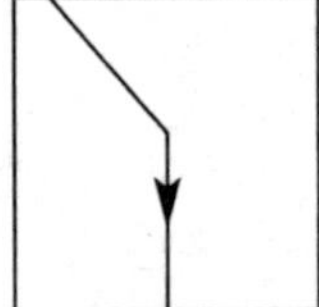

3.

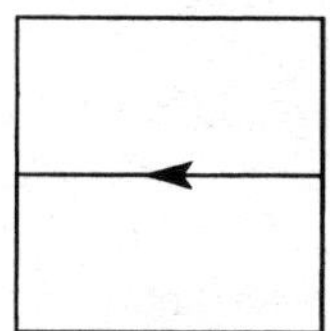

Exercise 2

1. court action
2. reminder sent
3. 60 days

Timed flow diagram exercise

1. letter of rejection sent
2. no further action
3. offer of post
4. applicant is invited to sit test
5. details of applicant are passed to management

3. Checking (pages 119–121)

Exercise 1

Those company names with errors have been placed in brackets.

Paine Chocolates	(Pain Chocolates)
Pall Mall Dispensing	Pall Mall Dispensing
Lodge Insurance Brokers	(Lodge Insurence Brokers)
Lodder Est Agts	(LOdder Est Agts)
Mill Hill Dry Clnrs	Mill Hill Dry Clnrs
Kahn Printers	Kahn Printers
Italian Piano Co	Italian Piano Co
Hoxtex Restaurants	(Hoxtex Restaurant)
Apollo Bed and Breakfast	(Apollo Bedand Breakfast)
Holloway Carpenters	Holloway Carpenters
Archway Halal Meat	(Archway Hala Meat)
Hookway Jewellers	Hookway Jewellers
Hi-tec School of Motoring	Hi-tec School of Motoring
Totland Hire Centre	(Totland Hire Center)

George's Recruitment	(Georges Recruitment)
West End Consultants	West End Consultants
Court Cars	(Court cars)
House of Lighting	(Hourse of Lighting)
Woxton Water Works	Woxton Water Works
Castletown Restaurants	(Castletown Recruitments)
Hardwood Doors Group Ltd	(Hardwood Doors Group LTD)
Mike's Do It Yourself Centre	Mike's Do It Yourself Centre
MITAKA Publishing House	(MITAKA Publsihing House)
Sunchung Takeaway	(Sanchung Takeaway)
Move Motorcycle Hire	(Move Motorcyycle Hire)
Portman Car and Van Rental	(Portman Carr and Van Rental)
Heitman and Son Accountants	(Heitman and son Accountance)
Ace Consulting Engineers	Ace Consulting Engineers
Hot Tandoori House	(Hot Tundoori House)
Safe Security Ltd	(Safe security Ltd)

Exercise 2

Original	*Copy*
ABC123	ABC123
ACCB/123/321	ACCB/123/321
CENTIMETRES/CUBIC	(CENTEMETRES/CUBIC)
GUMPTION	GUMPTION
MEASURES/CAPACITY	(MAESURES/CAPACITY)
987654321/123456789	987654321/123456789
987/123/654/456:	(987/123/654/456)
GERMANIUM-72.59	(GERMANUM-72.59)
MOLYBDENUM-95.94	MOLYBDENUM-95.94
NICKEL-58.71	(NICKLE-58.71)
ZIRCONIUM-91.22	ZIRCONIUM-91.22
PHOSPHORUS-30.9738	(PHOSPHOROS-30.9738)
MILLILITRES-36966	(MILLILITERS-36966)
MANGANESE-54.9380	MANGANESE-54.9380
DECAGRAMMES-15432	(DECAGRAMMS-15432)
KILOGRAMME-2205	(KILOGRAMMES-2205)
ANTIMONY-121.75	ANTIMONY-121.75
HYDROGEN-1.0080(H)	(HYDROGIN-1.0080(H))
CHROMIUM-51.996	(CHROMUIM-51.996)
MINNESOTA STATE	(MINNISOTA STATE)

ZEDEKIAH	ZEDEKIAH
WYOMING/CHEYENNE	(WYCOMING/CHEYENNE)
TENNESSEE/NASHVILLE	(TENESSEE/NASHVILLE)
ZOROASTER	ZOROASTER
PENNSYLVANIA/H'BURG	(PENNCYLVANIA/H'BURG)
WHISTLER	(WHISLER)
VERSAILLES	(VERSAILES)
VERRUCOSE	VERRUCOSE
UNHALLOWED	(UNIHALLOWED)
TREACHEROUS	TREACHEROUS
TREASURY	(TREASUERY)
SPARE-PART	(SPAIRE-PART)
ROUSSEAU	(RUOSSEAU)
EQUIVALENTS	(EQIUVALENTS)
FLOUNCE	(FLUONCE)
HARDENBERG	HARDENBERG

Exercise 3

Original	*Copy*
123/456/789/AC	123/456/789/AC
987/654/321/CA	987/654/321/CA
32323/452/CIC	(32332/452/CIC)
ACEG/818/658	ACEG/818/658
BDFH/4653/12	(BDFH)4653/12)
ZED/678/TLT/010	ZED/678/TLT/010
WORLD/VIEW/83	(WORLD/VEIW/83)
ZEBEDEE/F/JJ	(ZEBFDEE/F/JJ)
YETI/SNOW/MAN	YETI/SNOW/MAN
ORI/GIN/AL/212	ORI/GIN/AL/212
ADVERTISEMENT	(ADVERITISEMENT)
PERSONNEL/DEPT	(PERSENNEL/DEPT)
COM/PUT/ER/SYS/TEM	(COM/PUT/ER/SyS/TEM)
00/11/22/345/678	00/11/22/345/678
3456/0987/4321/32	3456/0987/4321/32
RO/AD/RU/NN/ER/234	(RO/AD/RV/NN/ER/234)
GAL/2001/200001/00	(GAL/2001/20001/00)
ISBN 0–561–15163–0	ISBN 0–561–15163–0
1010101/02020/300	1010101/02020/300
DATA-100/303/404/50	(DATA/100/303/404/50)

4. Following coded instructions (2) (pages 122–123)

1. [3]
2. [2]
3. [4]
4. [5]
5. [5]
6. [2]
7. [4]
8. [5]

5. Following coded instructions (3) (pages 124–125)

1. [3]
2. [1]
3. [2]
4. [3]
5. [5]
6. [2]
7. [2]
8. [4]
9. [2]
10. [1]

6. Sequencing (pages 126–129)

A. 2, 6, 7, 3, 1, 5, 4
B. 2, 3, 1, 4
C. 4, 2, 1, 3
D. 5, 3, 4, 2, 6, 1
E. 2, 4, 3, 1
F. 3, 2, 1
G. 4, 2, 3, 1
H. C
I. Nephew and Aunty
J. Due South

Further Reading from Kogan Page

Assert Yourself: How to do a Good Deal Better with Others, 2nd edition, Robert Sharpe, 1995

Career, Aptitude and Selection Tests: Match Your IQ, Personality and Abilities to Your Ideal Career, Jim Barrett, 1998

Get the Job You Want in 30 Days, Gary Joseph Grappo, 1998

Great Answers to Tough Interview Questions: How to Get the Job You Want, 4th edition, Martin John Yate, 1998

How to Master Personality Questionnaires: the Essential Guide, Mark Parkinson, 1997

How to Master Psychometric Tests: Winning Strategy for Test-takers, Mark Parkinson, 1997

How to Pass Computer Selection Tests, Sanjay Modha, 1994

How to Pass Graduate Recruitment Tests, Mike Bryon, 1994

How to Pass Numeracy Tests, Harry Tolley and Ken Thomas, 1996

How to Pass the Police Initial Recruitment Test, Harry Tolley, Ken Thomas and Catherine Tolley, 1997

How to Pass the Civil Service Qualifying Tests, Mike Bryon, 1995

How to Pass Technical Selection Tests, Mike Bryon and Sanjay Modha, 1993

How to Pass Verbal Reasoning Tests, Harry Tolley and Ken Thomas, 1996

The Image Factor: a Guide to Effective Self-presentation for Career Enhancement, 2nd edition, Eleri Sampson, 1996

Improving your Communication Skills, 2nd edition, Malcolm Peel, 1995

Interviews Made Easy: How to Get the Psychological Advantage, Mike Parkinson, 1994

Job-hunting Made Easy: a Step-by-step Guide, 3rd edition, John Bramham and David Cox, 1995

Learning Maps and Memory Skills: Powerful Techniques to Improve your Brain Power, 2nd edition, Ingemar Svantesson, 1997

Preparing Your Own CV: How to Improve Your Chances of Getting the Job You Want, Rebecca Corfield, 1990

Rate Yourself! Assess Your Skills, Personality and Abilities for the Job You Want, Marthe Sansregret and Dyane Adam, 1998

Readymade CVs: a Source Book for Job Hunters, Lynn Williams, 1996

Readymade Interview Questions, 2nd edition, Malcolm Peel, 1996

Readymade Job Search Letters: All the Letters You Need for a Successful Job Hunt, Lynn Williams, 1995

Successful Interview Skills, Rebecca Corfield, 1992

30 Minutes to Boost Your Self Esteem, Patricia Cleghorn, 1998

30 Minutes to Make the Right Impression, Eleri Sampson, 1997

30 Minutes Before Your Job Interview, June Lines, 1997

30 Minutes Before a Meeting, Alan Barker, 1997

30 Minutes to Boost Your Communication Skills, Elizabeth Tierney, 1997

30 Minutes to Prepare a Job Application, June Lines, 1997

Test Your Own Aptitude, 2nd edition, Jim Barrett and Geoff Williams, 1990

Working for Yourself: the Daily Telegraph Guide to Self Employment, Geoffrey Golzen, annual

Your First Job, 3rd edition, Vivien Donald and Ray Grosse, 1997